WORLD WAR I ARMY TRAINING *by* SAN FRANCISCO BAY

The Story of CAMP FREMONT

Barbara Wilcox

Published by The History Press
Charleston, SC
www.historypress.net

Front cover illustration: Detail from Political Poster Collection, US 5027, Hoover Institution Archives. *Courtesy of Hoover Institution Library and Archives, Stanford University.*
Back cover images: *Stanford Historical Photo Collection, Stanford University Archives.*

First published 2016

Manufactured in the United States

ISBN 978.1.46711.891.0

Library of Congress Control Number: 2015952926

CONTENTS

Acknowledgements 5
Introduction 7

1. Imperial San Francisco Goes to War 17
2. Trench and Campus: Stanford Rallies Around the Flag 45
3. War as Opportunity: Locals Find Roles in the Great Adventure 69
4. "He Will Come Back a Better Man!": Health and the 1918 Influenza Epidemic 83
5. Mapping the Future: How World War I Helped Shape the West 111

Notes 129
Bibliography 135
Index 141
About the Author 144

ACKNOWLEDGEMENTS

This little-known San Francisco Bay Area tale could not have been told without the help of many people. At Stanford University, I thank Professor David M. Kennedy of the Department of History, who read my work with the critical but forbearing eye of a great historian and a fine writer. Linda Paulson, associate dean and director of Stanford's Master of Liberal Arts program, expressed her confidence and support in myriad essential ways. Charles Junkerman and Stanford's Division of Continuing Studies funded my travel to the National Archives in Washington, D.C. Professor Peter Stansky and the Stanford Historical Society, particularly Laura Jones, Karen Bartholomew and Roxanne Nilan, recognized my project in its early stages and published a portion of the research. University archivist Daniel Hartwig and Tim Noakes and Mattie Taormina of the Stanford library's Department of Special Collections and University Archives provided invaluable help. Rusty Dolleman and Nazima Chowdhary made wise suggestions. Perhaps most of all, support from my classmates kept me going.

Kathy Restaino and the Menlo Park Historical Association shared letters, photos and scrapbooks from their collection by soldiers and nurses who fondly remembered their Camp Fremont days. Much of this historically valuable material is published here for the first time. Crystal Miles was of great help in the University of California–Berkeley's Bancroft Library. The Hoover Institution Archives at Stanford; the SLAC National Accelerator Laboratory's Archives and History Office; Filoli Center, Woodside, California; Nancy Lund and the Portola Valley

Historical Association; Bob Swanson; Curt and Christine Taylor; and Gary McMaster and the Camp Roberts Historical Museum all generously provided data that enhanced this work.

John Martin of San Diego, Will Lee of the U.S. Department of Veterans Affairs, Elena Reese, Dwight Harbaugh, Leslie Gordon and the late Tom Wyman generously shared their insights. John Spritzer, formerly of the U.S. Geological Survey, shared the desire to explore "Stanford's hidden World War I tunnels" that became the impetus of this project.

Dr. Nick Kanas and the California Map Society offered a speaking platform that was essential to conceptualizing the finished product. Megan Laddusaw at The History Press shepherded it through to completion.

Laurence Wilcox gave unflagging good humor and support.

Many other people gave help, advice and support—too many to name, but I thank them all.

INTRODUCTION

Not many homes in the Palo Alto hills have swimming pools. The foothills, especially in winter, are cooler than one might expect, with breeze from the Golden Gate reaching the region by afternoon and sending its tempering breath over the rolling grasslands and venerable oak trees. People in Silicon Valley think of themselves as doers, in any event, not as loungers by pools. For an invigorating swim, which is more in tune with how locals live, the Palo Alto Hills Golf and Country Club is down the street. But the client wanted a house with a pool, and so the contractor brought in equipment one morning in November 2010 and started, cautiously, to dig.

Pretty soon, the blade began unearthing hunks of long, rusty shells, deeply corroded, dozens of them, many with marble-sized shrapnel balls still nestled inside. A ringing *ping* of metal on metal heralded each new find. The contractor had heard this might happen and slowed the work pace even further. Then a blade connected with an object that made a distinctly thicker, robust *thunk*, and a bomb squad was called in.

This crew had encountered some of the few remaining physical traces of Camp Fremont, a World War I U.S. Army training camp that claimed roughly sixty-eight thousand acres of the San Francisco Peninsula, from San Carlos to Los Altos, at its peak in summer 1918. The camp's nucleus was seven thousand acres leased from Stanford University and from private, mostly absentee, owners in what is now the small city of Menlo Park, where the camp was headquartered. It was one of thirty-two camps designated to train an army vastly enlarged after America's April 1917 war declaration.

Sixteen of these camps, including Fremont, had to be hurriedly built from the ground up. At Camp Fremont's peak, more than twenty-eight thousand men of the army's newly formed Eighth Division trained there for combat on the Western Front. They practiced trench warfare on a maneuver ground, complete with dugouts and underground galleries, on the site of today's Stanford Linear Accelerator Center (SLAC) National Laboratory south of Sand Hill Road. They used an artillery range, where the crew digging a swimming pool found the unexploded shell in November 2010, stretching coastward from the Stanford property now called Dish Hill into the forested slopes between Los Trancos and Madera Creeks. There, on what now largely remains open space, men of Camp Fremont's Eighth Field Artillery Brigade spent a few intense weeks firing seventy-five-millimeter field guns from Dish Hill into the type of reverse slopes they hoped soon to conquer on the Western Front. It is ammunition from such a "French 75"—quick and accurate, the famed workhorse of the Allies—that excavators still occasionally find in the Palo Alto foothills today. Likewise, trenches and dugouts of Camp Fremont emerge after heavy rains as sinkholes among today's research installations and venture-capital firms. They are palimpsests from an earlier era of growth, innovation and change.

Few men who trained at Camp Fremont actually saw action in the Great War. Stationed on the West Coast, days by rail from the Atlantic ports of embarkation, the Eighth was the last of the American Expeditionary Force's (AEF) divisions to be put on trains before the November 11, 1918 Armistice. Some Camp Fremont units reached Europe in time to help with the occupation of defeated Germany or to build facilities for the AEF's return to the United States. Most got no farther than the Atlantic docks when peace broke out. That August, five thousand Camp Fremont men had been stripped from the Eighth Division and shipped across the Pacific Ocean to Vladivostok, Siberia, where they were kept until early 1920 as part of President Woodrow Wilson's failed Russian intervention to check Bolshevism there. Training draftees to fill their ranks probably contributed to the delay in Camp Fremont's deployment.

The strange tale of America's Siberian intervention has been told elsewhere and is largely outside the scope of this book. Camps like Fremont, however, remain largely unexplored, both as physical places and as historical phenomena. Because Camp Fremont was evanescent, fading like most of its sister training camps into America's postwar landscape, it is easy to dismiss as a curiosity. "The tunnels" of the trench maneuver ground are remembered fondly but with little sense of context by many locals, now elderly, who played in them as boys before Stanford sealed them in the 1940s. Yet the tunnels have a story to tell.

Camp Fremont and its sister camps across the nation uniquely reveal how America mobilized to win a war in which most citizens had little personally at stake and further reveal how the scope and totality of that mobilization changed many Americans' lives. Support for the war was not unanimous or selfless, despite wartime images of patriotic parades and families happily eating unfamiliar foods to save wheat and meat for the fighting men. In fact, World War I America was a tense place. The war was controversial and often widened existing rifts. A close look at Camp Fremont shows us this.

Federal power soared in the seventeen months the United States was at war—power to tax, power to spend, power to control corporate and individual behavior in ways large and small. Yet the U.S. war relied at least as much on Americans' voluntary efforts. It relied on mobilizing the will of the people to accept controversial measures such as the military draft. It relied on voluntarism to fulfill the war effort in ways Congress would not or could not compel, such as getting localities to provide the large tracts of land required for camps like Fremont. At the same time, the government had to soothe locals' well-founded concerns about the vice that in past wars had followed soldiers wherever they went.

Troops kept pets in camp and smuggled them overseas when they could. *Bob Swanson collection.*

The government appealed where it could to blatant self-interest, the line of least resistance. It also appealed to the implied self-interest of altruism, of the benefit through affiliation to the greater good that was a keystone of the age's progressive thinking. Next, and again using the progressive toolkit, government worked the levers of public opinion and mass psychology to shape Americans' behavior in support of war aims. Finally, government enhanced its own power to police, to evict and to detain. The scope and consequence of the U.S. war effort, as well as the mindset that made it possible, are clearest where the mobilization was physically concentrated, including the army training camps like Fremont that sprung up across the nation in late 1917. When the people of the San Francisco Peninsula welcomed Camp Fremont into their oak-studded foothills, they invited government into their lives in a new and pervasive way. Whether the experience made them happy rested largely on whether they thought they had reaped the rewards that the government had promised, whether they believed the propaganda and how well they negotiated new roles in this changing world.

It seems odd now that a university, let alone a coeducational university in a more genteel era, would welcome an army division of lusty young soldiers onto precincts roughly a quarter of a mile from its women's dormitory. It seems preposterous—decades after Vietnam-era protest severed links between defense contracting and academia at many universities, including Stanford—that a university would allow field guns onto its precincts for the purpose of shelling neighboring properties, however sparsely settled the ground. Just as oddly, Camp Fremont was brought to rural San Mateo and Santa Clara Counties by a group led by the mayor of the city and county of San Francisco, someone whose legal authority ended thirty miles north of camp and whose attempts to similarly dictate land use outside his jurisdiction would today be strenuously fought if not instantly shut down.

In fact, none of these moves found unanimous favor in 1917–18. "Problems of interrelations" among soldiers and local women, in a Stanford official's words, caused strife both in the university and in town. Federal and local officials shadowed and investigated women they found consorting with troops at Camp Fremont and elsewhere. Many Stanford women resented the university's harsh—and, as it turned out, futile—new rules imposed to keep them away from the soldiers whom public opinion praised so much. As for the artillery bombardments, one downrange landowner's opposition may have figured into the army's decision to move Camp Fremont's gunners to Fort Sill, Oklahoma, after only a few weeks. But it is important to realize that the camp and its guns and its rules found favor with the majority. They offered proof that their formerly sleepy area was progressive and patriotic and was doing its part to win America's first global war.

Historian David Kennedy identified the real Great War waged in the United States as a "war for the American mind." Kennedy's 1980 book *Over Here* traces how the Wilson administration harnessed the progressive ideology so popular at the time to win support for a less popular war effort. In its broadest terms, progressivism sought the use of government and institutions for the common good. It arose to correct a perceived excess of individualism that shaded into selfishness, whether among industrial trusts abusing corporate power or among a populace lacking common and binding purpose. The problem was that an ideology that exalted the common good also yielded motive and means to coerce the individual. This happened by law, the draft itself being the most notable example. It also happened via public opinion that was heavily shaped by government propaganda, law being considered more autocratic and therefore less desirable than consensus in the progressive mindset. While the government did not intend to incite hysteria, an effort driven by popular opinion gave outliers little legal remedy or standing to say "no." Carried to extremes by the need for total mobilization, the result was a paradox, as California progressive leader Senator Hiram Johnson warned: "[I]n our tenderness for democracy abroad, we forgot democracy at home." War doubters had to self-censor or face arrest. Neighbors browbeat one another to buy Liberty bonds or to do more on behalf of the soldiers. Conscientious objectors were threatened with baths of excrement. All these seedy doings emerged in and around Camp Fremont.[1]

Progressives reasoned that camps like Fremont introduced troops to many features of America's twentieth-century urbanization. The camps gave many soldiers their first taste of life in large, complex groups, of dental care and vaccination, of competitive team sports, of household electricity and, if their units were among the few linked to Camp Fremont's hard-won sewer line, of modern plumbing. Progressives drove the War Department's often-coercive efforts to guard soldiers' sexual health and to prevent camps like Fremont from becoming hotbeds of vice. They drove public health efforts to stem the 1918 flu epidemic, which swept through Camp Fremont during the global mobilization and ultimately claimed millions of lives. Progressivism even influenced army training itself and helped to paper over that training's shortcomings. Finally, progressive ideas of civic improvement help explain why Camp Fremont ended up where it did and how it affected people both on base and nearby.

The War Department appealed to self-interest where it could. The San Francisco civic and business leaders who lobbied Washington for a camp did so

The war ended before most Camp Fremont men sailed. This cartoonist from Fremont's Twelfth Infantry was not alone in his disappointment. *From* The Twelfth U.S. Infantry—Its Story by Its Men.

to further a "Greater San Francisco," a regional entity in fact if not by statute, one that assured progress and stability in an area far beyond their jurisdiction but whose resources, such as water and electricity, they largely controlled. Like the Hetch Hetchy water system then being planned and the 1915 Panama-Pacific International Exposition, Camp Fremont involved many of the same prominent players. It meant to maintain the regional economic dominance of the city that historian Judd Kahn and geographer Gray Brechin dubbed "Imperial San Francisco." The civic bigwigs, in turn, marketed the project to smaller-scale Peninsula real estate interests who welcomed the infrastructure, especially sewers, that they thought an army camp would bring.

The motives of Stanford University, then young, land-poor and struggling for identity, are more oblique. Trustees hoped leasing six thousand acres for an army camp would prove Stanford's patriotism against the activities of its pacifist ex-president, David Starr Jordan, whose barnstorming against war was raining negative publicity on the university. Wartime university president Ray Lyman Wilbur, unlike his predecessors, was among those who thought national service would improve America's youth. Insights that

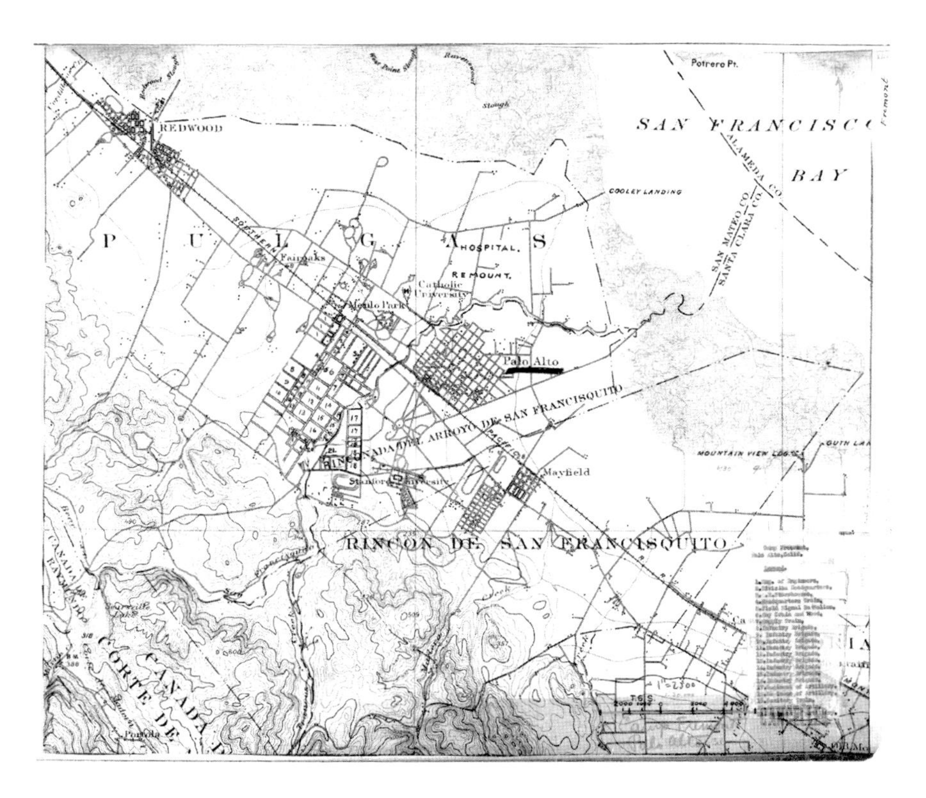

Camp Fremont as planned by the army in 1917. Menlo Park, where the camp was headquartered, was then an unincorporated community of some 2,300 people. *National Archives.*

Wilbur gained from friend and Stanford trustee Herbert Hoover—who was fast gaining world prominence through his relief efforts for civilians caught in the conflict—lent immediacy in Wilbur's eyes to the faraway war and grounded a conviction he expressed hotly to War Secretary Newton D. Baker in May 1917 "that unless something is done, and done very promptly, we are going to be spending our time after this war…in raking together a big indemnity" against Allied loss and suffering.[2]

Still, many Americans did not understand why the United States entered the distant conflict. Many, like Jordan, did not buy into Wilson's stated plan to "make the world safe for democracy." The army major recruiting up and down California for Camp Fremont's 319th Engineer Regiment in January 1918 encountered sheer puzzlement and often a language barrier, particularly in cities swollen with unassimilated immigrants: Why was there a war? Why did it need engineers? Before the war, most Americans' contact with federal government stopped at the local post office. An income tax had been imposed four years earlier, but only an affluent few were liable to pay. Americans had little sense and little evidence of their vast and diverse nation as a monumental entity, much less as the shaper of world geopolitics that Wilson aimed for the United States to become. Here, too, progressive thought was harnessed to unify and inspire the people. Men of Camp Fremont's 12th Infantry Regiment, mostly draftees, saw themselves in the progressive manner as ragtag citizens molded by government into a better whole. "When a good compound...finds its way to the market everyone is interested in it," one infantryman wrote in tellingly impersonal fashion. "Uncle Sam had put into existence such a new article...THE AMERICAN SOLDIER."[3]

This new wartime relationship with government was not one of equals, a fact obvious in the twenty-first century but much less so at the time. As the war effort grew larger, some individuals chafed at the terms. Stanford did not intend, and the army did not disclose, upon securing Camp Fremont's lease in mid-1917, that an artillery range and all the trouble it generated would soon arise near campus. Camp Fremont consumed not just land but also Stanford staff and students, classes and programs; it was a "great military university," in one local businessman's sanguine view, competing with the actual university it partly occupied. The camp's Menlo Park lessors, for their part, were dismayed to learn the army had no intention of gifting their poorly draining land with the sewerage that the state mandated for development in the area. The issue delayed camp building and occupation until funds for sewerage could be found. Stanford, for its part, worked to redefine itself in the wake of the war, undergoing financial restructuring, among other changes.

Just as Stanford and its neighbors reveal how civilians navigated their new relationship with government, two Camp Fremont units, the 12th Infantry and 319th Engineers, show how America's citizen-soldiers struggled to find meaning in their roles in a war that ended before they could fight in it. For many, failure to reach the battlefield was a crushing disappointment, one they shared with more than half the four million Americans under arms at war's end. Camp Fremont's infantrymen and engineers explain their experience in two different ways that illustrate the paradigm progressivism imposed on the war. While the infantrymen saw their worth in affiliation to the larger whole, forged in the progressive crucible, the engineers gained material rather than primarily ideological benefits from war service. As a unit, they were better educated than average, and their army training accentuated these differences. They gained project-management and mapping skills that allowed them, especially in retrospect, to see themselves as exceptional individuals.

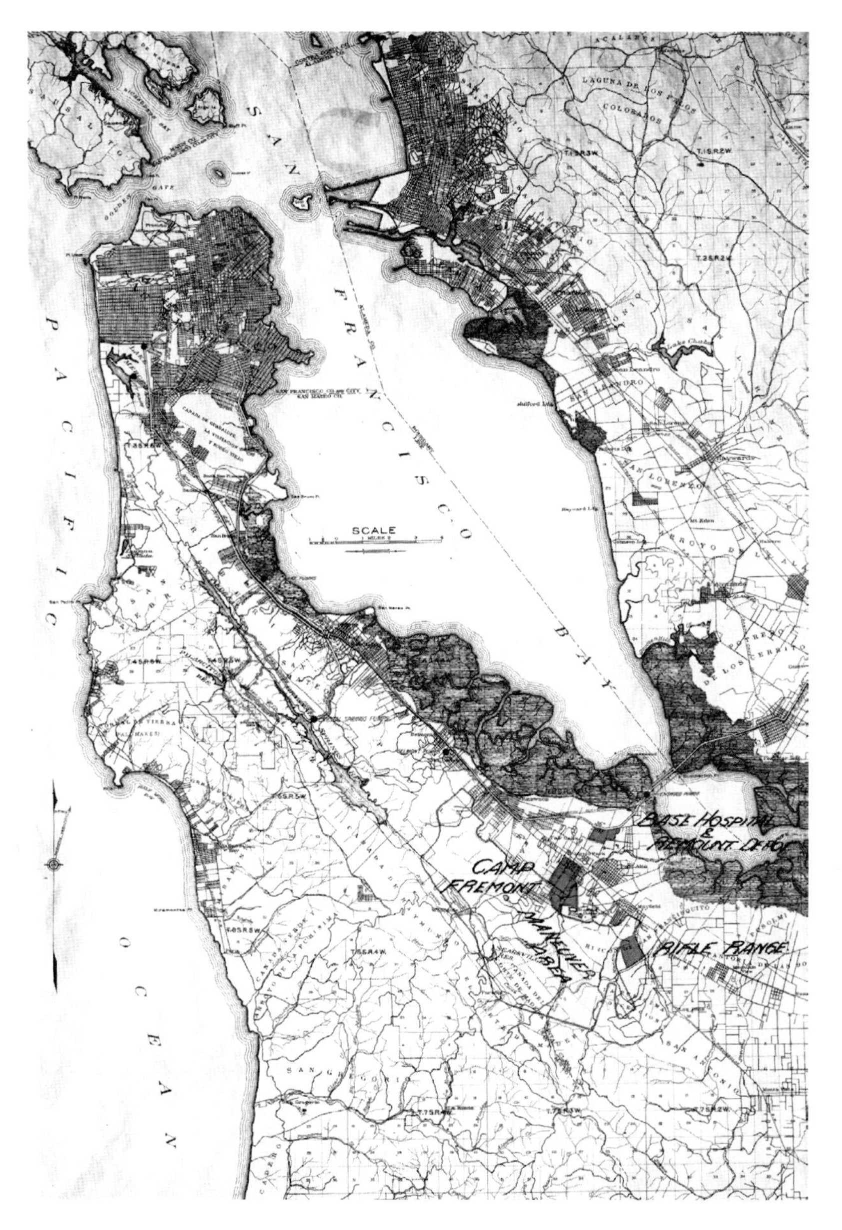

The camp and its maneuver grounds ultimately took up more than sixty-eight thousand acres of the mid-Peninsula, as shown on this 1918 army map. *National Archives.*

Many went on to make significant contributions to U.S. science and engineering. They helped develop the West and contributed to the growth that now all but obliterates Camp Fremont's physical traces.

These men of the 319th glamorized their thrice-weekly bayonet drill, though, like much of the training, it was a relic of past wars. *Menlo Park Historical Association.*

A look at Camp Fremont's hospital reveals the ubiquity of infectious disease in early twentieth-century America and the hope of camp healthcare workers that mobilization would spread public health reforms. Fire destroyed part of the wood-frame hospital in September 1918, three weeks before the influenza epidemic reached the Bay Area. Astonishingly, the fire caused no casualties, despite the camp's low building standards and lack of fire protection. The episode reveals the mobilization's haphazardness as men spent months crammed into flimsy quarters meant for a few weeks. It reveals that the worth the army assigned to its soldiers' health and safety was not absolute, as the government maintained, but rested on their shipment overseas to become weapons of war.

What all these people and entities had in common was that they were forced to redefine themselves under new and trying conditions. Some were heroes. Some were rebels. Some internalized their dissent or quietly went AWOL. Most were foot soldiers or behind-the-scenes helpers. Some were beneficiaries. Some, arguably, were victims. All learned for the first time to define themselves in relation to federal authority. Camp Fremont reveals how progressive notions of power, authority and modernity shaped the U.S. World War I mobilization. One heritage of the war was that Americans were left, for good or ill, to live in relation to a government grown massively larger. This book examines Camp Fremont in terms of how it changed the landscape and the lives of the people in and around it, both soldiers and civilians. In so doing, it opens a window into how World War I helped to change America a century ago.

Chapter 1

IMPERIAL SAN FRANCISCO GOES TO WAR

As James Rolph Jr., mayor of the city and county of San Francisco, left his city hall office on the afternoon of April 24, 1917, he stepped forth into a civic center built largely on his watch that would be, despite waves of redevelopment, familiar today. Rolph's Beaux-Arts city hall still stands, made even fancier by later accretions of gilt and glitz. So does the nearby Civic Auditorium, where, amid great pageantry that afternoon, Rolph spoke at a ceremony bestowing U.S. flags on groups of college volunteers leaving to become civilian ambulance drivers in the faraway world war. Twelve thousand well-wishers filled the auditorium for the volunteers' departure. Both the ceremony and a large part of the men's expenses were underwritten by the Friends of France, wealthy advocates of U.S. entrance into the war.

The Friends were led by William Bowers Bourn II, owner of the Empire gold mine and president of San Francisco's water system, who soon would help to site Camp Fremont near his country home then rising on the Peninsula. Silver plaques on each flagpole labeled the flags as gifts of the American League of California, whose chairman was Ray Lyman Wilbur, the new president of Stanford University. The league's goal was "to ensure unanimous and unquestioning loyalty to the nation in the prosecution of those measures which will be necessary for the successful conduct of the war." The Stanford and University of California volunteers bore the flags to the front as symbols of support for the Allies, whose cause America had formally joined with its declaration of war three weeks earlier. The flags' symbolic power foreshadowed the famous boast, "Lafayette, we are here," uttered by a U.S. officer at the marquis' grave as the first troops of the American Expeditionary Force marched in Paris on July 4.[4]

Support for the distant war had lately risen in the San Francisco Bay Area, as in the nation generally, particularly after Germany's resumption in February of unrestricted submarine warfare against Allied and neutral ships. No one claimed this support was unanimous, especially in San Francisco. Although the West's leading port city had always hosted military bases and a robust defense industry, the long run-up to America's April 6 war declaration cleft San Francisco and exposed deep socioeconomic rifts. City labor leaders—not just radicals like the Industrial Workers of the World but also the moderate and much more politically connected Building Trades Council—believed war only benefited military contractors. Many such contractors made fortunes even as America remained neutral, including Rolph himself, a shipbuilder and shipper of lumber and other Allied needs. When the British liner *Lusitania* was sunk by a German torpedo in 1915 en route from New York to Liverpool, it carried not just American passengers but also more than six million rounds of Remington .303 rifle ammunition procured in the United States for the Allied cause. In practical terms, trade and lending cost America its neutrality long before the war declaration as the British blockade and German depredations swung U.S. investment to the Allied side. Other Americans raged as they watched the nation prepare, as they saw it, to shed blood for these rich men's assets. Nine months before the April flag ceremony, a nail bomb placed by unknown culprits shattered the San Francisco Chamber of Commerce's Preparedness Day Parade down Market Street. Ten people were killed and more than forty injured in what remains one of America's deadliest acts of mass violence. Rolph led that parade as well.

Rolph's support of the war was leavened by his unusual rapport with the ordinary people whose young men his city would send to fight in it. A charismatic populist, a social liberal, a progressive and a friend of labor, as well as a self-made millionaire who remained in the humble Mission District where he was born, "Sunny Jim," as he was known, strove in his twenty years as mayor to reconcile the city's contesting factions of capital and labor, vice and respectability, rich and poor. He frequently emptied his pockets for the down-at-heels who thronged outside his office, and when urged to curtail the vibrant economic sector that was prostitution in his city, he famously asked, "But what will be done with all the women put out of work?" Soldiers he met sent him missives from the front as if he were a relative and returned with disassembled machine guns smuggled aboard troop transports as gifts for their friend in city hall.[5]

San Franciscans honor departing civilian ambulance volunteers on April 24, 1917, with a ceremony in Civic Auditorium. *From* The Story of the First Flag.

Rolph is sometimes dismissed as a shaker of hands and a kisser of babies, a charming lightweight who left substance to others. Yet his popularity helped the city build extraordinary public works, including, eventually, the Hetch Hetchy project that flooded a valley in Yosemite National Park to bring water across the state to San Francisco. In 1917, the latest, and least controversial, of these great projects was the glittering Panama-Pacific International Exposition held two years earlier. It celebrated the city's rebuilding from near-destruction in the 1906 earthquake and fire, as well as the opening of the Panama Canal that brought the city further trade and military spending. The San Franciscans who lobbied Congress for the right to host the fair lobbied just as hard for federal projects in and beyond the city's hilly and geographically circumscribed forty-nine square miles. These included the U.S. Army Corps of Engineers' 1910 Dumbarton rail bridge to the south, of great portent as San Francisco Bay's first vehicular crossing. They included the future Hunters Point Naval Shipyard for the proposed Pacific Fleet that San Francisco wanted badly to host, as well as the Moffett Naval Air Station that Rolph helped to site in Santa Clara County a few years later. All such

Populist, progressive San Francisco mayor James Rolph Jr. thought creating jobs throughout the Bay Area would enhance social stability. *Library of Congress.*

enterprise, in Rolph's eyes at least, did more than enrich its sponsors. It created jobs and forestalled unrest born of scarcity, a fear common in the early twentieth century as socialism gained traction in Europe and America. As one labor leader put it at a Rolph campaign rally: "What's the use of a high wage if you don't have any work?"[6]

Camp Fremont, though thirty miles from the city, was planned by the leading men of San Francisco, the men who, "as a group, raise all the money for such purposes," said the *San Francisco Chronicle*, whose publisher, M.H. de Young, was among them. Camp Fremont represented not just patriotism but also "the interest of our prosperity," as de Young put it during the contentious and barely successful fundraising drive that hosting the camp would require. The trouble civic leaders had in raising the funds reveals that the unity the fair proclaimed was fraying two years later. Pressures of growth, change and San Francisco's own ever-expanding plans and consequent demands on taxpayers exposed the fragility of any common cause the city might proclaim. The war exacerbated these pressures.[7]

Many thoughtful people, including Wilbur and Bourn, hoped that exactly the opposite would happen. They hoped that war, or at least war training, would unify the nation. They believed that mobilization would enforce on Americans a common purpose, and that universal military service would homogenize its diverse population into something resembling a lost ideal. In some ways their hopes were realized, but the unity was transient and often a creature of propaganda to fulfill war aims, of sentiment dictated from above. In early 1917, as war exposed rifts in the city and society, the leaders of the San Francisco Bay Area strove to restore the unity and maintain the prosperity manifested in the glittering Panama-

Pacific fair. Rolph strove to remain, as his campaign slogan held, "Mayor of All the People." Arcing above the ambitions of Rolph and his peers were the similar but far more sophisticated goals of a federal government also seeking to unify Americans. Through Camp Fremont, the federal government used Rolph's efforts to serve not just his own constituents but also those in his city's sphere of regional influence to mobilize for war.

Within days of Congress's April 6 war declaration, the government began steps to greatly enlarge, equip and train an army that, unlike the U.S. Navy, was poorly equipped and very small. The U.S. Regular Army, excluding the even more poorly equipped National Guard, numbered fewer than 120,000 men. This was about the size of the Belgian regular army that Germany swept aside before invading France. It was less than thirty-nine days' worth of British casualties that spring at Arras, 120 miles northwest of what would become the Western Front's American sector. President Wilson aimed not just to win the war but also to leverage the win into a leading U.S. role at the peace talks. He needed a force large enough to sustain itself in a theater of grim attrition, autonomous enough that its role in victory would be clear.

German leaders knew America's size and wealth but also its unpreparedness. They benefited that spring from several developments, especially the resumption on February 1 of unrestricted submarine warfare, which the high command knew would incite U.S. wrath but, it gambled, could shorten the war by choking off Allied supplies. Germany's strategic withdrawal that spring to its Hindenburg Line reduced the line it had to defend while ceding relatively little to France, because troops destroyed everything of use as they fell back. The German high command figured it had a year to secure victory before the United States could send enough troops to reweight the scales. In fact, fifteen months elapsed between the U.S. war declaration and the landing in France of the first million troops in the four-million-man army that Wilson envisioned. U.S. bureaucrats and commanders stumbled at first as they built a war machine.

An early order of business, after Wilson signed the Selective Service Act on May 18, 1917, was the siting and building of camps to hold this new citizen army of draftees. Each camp was scaled for an army division, then twenty-eight thousand officers and men. Sixteen camps nationwide would house an expanded Regular Army and a new National Army of draftees. Sixteen flimsier and more temporary camps were built for an expanded and federalized National Guard. The former were to last the duration of the war and receive waves of fresh inductees, while the Guard was to leave for

Union Iron Works, founded in 1849 and acquired by Bethlehem in 1905, led San Francisco's robust war-contracting industry from its plant near Potrero Hill. *National Park Service.*

France as soon as its basic training was completed. The personnel distinction blurred even before the forces were unified in August 1918 as deployments were delayed and units were moved among camps. The construction hierarchy remained. Camps born as Regular Army camps boasted wooden barracks, sewerage and flush toilets. Camps born as National Guard camps made do with tents and privies. Fremont was a National Guard camp, to its boosters' belated understanding and lasting chagrin.

The War Department did not publicize this distinction in its progressivism-tinged portrayal of all the camps as "model cities" that would not only fit draftees to fight but also shape them into modern citizens—clean, vaccinated and conversant with American language, culture and ideals. Improved health, sanitation and civic literacy of the kind the camps seemed to offer were goals of the progressive movement. Americans were primed to seize such an offer, for the nation was urbanizing even as many of its intellectuals praised a vanishing idyll of rural life. The 1910 census was the last in which Americans were predominantly rural. For many draftees, camp would be the largest concentration of humanity in which they had ever lived. For perhaps half, it would be their first home with electricity.

Localities across America lobbied Washington for camps that the government blatantly promoted as development opportunities. Many cities got a head start during the prewar preparedness era as the army enacted a congressional mandate to slowly increase troop strength starting in 1916. General Franklin Bell told an enthusiastic San Diego Chamber of Commerce late that year that the projected annual economic impact of a base there would be $7 million to $9 million. That figure would rise with America's entrance into the war. Selection criteria included proximity to railroads; warm climate, since the government aimed to save money by housing as many men as possible in tents; and at least twenty-five thousand acres for maneuvers and drill, ideally in terrain like that of the Western Front. The government paid to build the camps at cost plus 10 percent, using firms recommended by local civilian advisers. Localities were expected to provide the land. In return, each camp locality reaped the

The 319th Engineers recruit in downtown Los Angeles. *Menlo Park Historical Association.*

benefits of a soldier payroll and procurement budget that one officer in the army's Western Division headquarters in San Francisco estimated at $2.25 million a month. It also received whatever army-built infrastructure was left behind—roads, water and electric lines, as well as sewers if applicable.

Voters in Pierce County, Washington, passed a $2 million bond issue to procure sixty-one thousand acres that became Camp Lewis, outside Tacoma. San Diego, which had pursued an army base since late 1915, offered eight thousand acres at the edge of town at $1 per year that became Camp Kearny. Louisville, Kentucky, gave the site of Camp Taylor rent-free. Lawton, Oklahoma, signed over its federal water right to the army to ensure sufficient water for Camp Doniphan.

San Francisco could do none of these things. The city was surrounded on three sides by ocean and bay, and suitable tracts of open land were outside its jurisdiction. It had little time to sell bonds and no confidence that voters would approve them. Already, voters had spurned the first of several bond issues for the Hetch Hetchy project. Instead, San Francisco worked its back channels, plumbing the interests of its business community and the resources it controlled beyond the city limits. Behind closed city hall doors, in June 1917, Rolph convened a committee of industrialists and civic leaders to strategize a Bay Area training camp. Those present included Sam Eastman, vice-president of Bourn's Spring Valley Water Co., which would provide the camp's water; John A. Britton, general manager of Pacific Gas and Electric Co., which would supply the electricity; financier Herbert Fleishhacker; and publisher de Young. They looked down the Peninsula to Bourn and Spring Valley, to Ray Lyman Wilbur and Stanford and to a prescient real estate developer named Walter Hoag. These men's reasons for hosting Camp Fremont reveal more clearly than could any more straightforward transaction the complexity of the motivations and tensions that America tapped to wage its first global war.

The way the San Francisco elite of Rolph's era controlled resources beyond the city limits is difficult to appreciate today. It arose in part from the speed with which relatively few newcomers to the Pacific coast's first U.S. metropolis aggregated land and power. It arose in part from geography. San Francisco was dry, dune-swept and hemmed in by ocean and bay. Its nearest source for arable land, for timber and most crucially for potable water was San Mateo County on the Peninsula to the south. This fact governed relations between the counties well into the twentieth century. City grandees summered at country estates to the south, keeping San Mateo County as a *contado* or controllable hinterland, in Brechin's analogy of imperial Venice, that they could simultaneously exalt and exploit. Clerk-assessor's maps of San Mateo County from 1909 and 1927 show individual tracts' owners, and in almost any square-mile segment more than half the owners of record—often all of them—are people resident in, or doing business in, San Francisco.

The county line remained notional as long as San Francisco had ten times the population of its southern neighbor and more bank clearings than the six next largest West Coast cities combined. Rolph placed, or was perceived to place, politicians friendly to the city and its causes in as many suburban legislative districts as he could. His reach during the Camp Fremont era is demonstrated by his city clerk's report to an army adjutant on when Rolph's committee would pay, as promised, the property taxes of several San Mateo County landowners who had provided camp land. The latter county's assessor "hopes, in fact, to bring about a reduction" in the tax rate so that the committee would have to pay less: "The county officials are at all times willing to cooperate." It helped that Rolph was hostile to Prohibition, then looming, and therefore a friend of many of San Mateo County's most cherished small businesses. The county's rurality hid revelry that less tolerant minds would use the war and the camp to squelch.[8]

San Francisco tried several times to amalgamate with its *contado* in law as well as fact, to form a "Greater San Francisco" with a borough system like that of New York. After the city persuaded Congress in 1913 to encroach on Yosemite National Park for its ambitious water plan, San Mateo County

The camp was run in many ways as an administrative outholding of San Francisco, with its mail handled by a branch of the city post office. *Bob Swanson collection.*

E.F. Fitzpatrick ran several enterprises from this Redwood City block, including the Camp Fremont leases he managed on behalf of James Rolph. *Author photo.*

voters began to chafe in harness. They understood that they were being groomed to help support the costly project. Suspicion rose as city leaders floated early studies of what became the Dumbarton and Bay auto bridges, framing them as joint ventures and splitting study costs equally though San Francisco was far richer. By the spring of 1917, as Rolph led a final bid for amalgamation, a banker in Redwood City, Judge E.F. Fitzpatrick, marshaled a Preservation League of San Mateo County to fight what a local paper called Rolph's "vicious legislation." Fitzpatrick was agreeable on other issues, though. He belonged to Wilbur's pro-war American League, as did several Stanford trustees. Rolph chose Fitzpatrick, his erstwhile foe, to wrangle the leases of the land that he formally offered the army for Camp Fremont on June 25, 1917, far outside his jurisdiction in San Mateo and Santa Clara Counties.[9]

In co-opting his opponent, Rolph aimed to demonstrate that affiliation with himself and with the city remained profitable. It is not irrelevant that Rolph ran for governor the next year. He aimed to provide, via Fitzpatrick and the army, modern infrastructure that the age praised and that many San Mateo County residents wanted but would not or could not pay for. He could ensure these locals' loyalty by creating an instant market of twenty-eight thousand soldiers for their "cigar stores and pie counters," as his city clerk put it—small businesses that did not foreclose on San Mateo County's continuing to be a rural resource shed for the city. By bringing Camp Fremont to the Peninsula, Rolph could demonstrate his own continued benevolence and that of San Francisco, the self-styled Queen City of the West.

Meanwhile, Bourn waited for city voters to cease rejecting the bond measures that would take Spring Valley off his hands, complete Hetch Hetchy and place the combined water system under the ownership of the people of San Francisco. He looked for new investments, for cultural projects and for causes. An Anglophile who had sailed at least once (in 1910) on the *Lusitania*, Bourn had other links that predisposed him to support the Allies, including a Cambridge education, an English son-in-law and an Anglo-Irish estate. He evinced his philosophy of business, as well as of public relations, to his attorney in 1918 as he mulled one of his periodic libel threats against the *Chronicle*, which fought Spring Valley's every move: "To many we seem a grasping corporation endeavouring to take advantage of every technicality to hold up their rate payers. I believe we are only trying to get what we believe the law intends to allow us."[10]

The war opened Bourn's heart and his wallet. He believed with many Americans that the nation was losing its edge to prosperity and to excessive individualism, in part because a spike in immigration at the turn of the twentieth century meant many residents no longer had a common heritage. The progressive intellectual Herbert Croly articulated this fear in his 1909 *The Promise of American Life* as a "drift" from shared values into rootlessness. Croly's take on the national ennui was promulgated by Theodore Roosevelt, whom Bourn admired greatly, and joined a skein of thought that found a solution to America's woes in war. Maneuvers and drill would toughen both the disadvantaged immigrant and the effete old stock. Universal military service would homogenize so-called hyphenated Americans into what holders of this view called a "re-created" nation. In this view, shared by Bourn and others, the United States declared war not only on Germany but also on its own weakness.

"Great disaster to America is synonymous with the general acceptance of the word 'prosperity,'" Bourn wrote. "I am almost of the opinion that the standards of my country America are being commercialized, and would gladly welcome any condition that could re-create us into a nation with the ideals and standards of our forebears." He made his case in a stirring speech before ten thousand people at the Panama-Pacific International Exhibition's "Day of France and Belgium" on November 27, 1915:

> *The soul of France was born and dwells in Idealism. It was from the germ of French idealism that sprang the soul of America. When materialism breaks itself against the mighty walls of an ideal—a nation will be saved from being a people without a soul. Efficiency, wealth, material comfort, appeal to all; but they cannot produce…the glory that France now dwells in.* Is America neutral?

Charcoal sketch of William Bowers Bourn II by John Singer Sargent, 1915. *Courtesy of Filoli Center, Woodside, California.*

It was an odd appeal coming from someone who owned a gold mine, but it touched a nerve. The crowd roared back: "*No! No!*"[11]

Bourn funded several Allied causes including the civilian ambulance drivers, who freed Allied nationals for combat roles. He was drawn to the latter by Joseph Eastman, a Stanford junior and would-be driver whose older brother, Sam Eastman, was Spring Valley's vice-president. Most drivers were affluent college men or young graduates, and most paid their own way. They shared with many preparedness advocates a conviction that a nation's elite was best fitted and first called to defend the nation's honor, rather than a separate military caste. General Leonard Wood set the tone by exhorting Harvard men to form a well-born fighting corps reminiscent of the English public school heroes who were prodigiously offering their lives. Bourn loved the pageantry of the ambulance service, the young men's exchange of flags and high-flown vows, and thought it, too, filled a heart's need.

Perhaps because this work placed Bourn in Wilbur's orbit, perhaps because Spring Valley director Frank Anderson was already on Stanford's Board of Trustees, Bourn joined the Stanford board in mid-1917. There, he helped to commit America's largest contiguous university property to the war.

Wilbur's friend and university trustee Herbert Hoover was Stanford's best-known graduate, a mining engineer and investor plunged by a chance trip to Europe into war relief and public life. Hoover was on Panama-Pacific International Exposition business in London when war broke out in August 1914. He began by repatriating fellow Americans stranded by the conflict. Soon he was managing relief for an entire Belgian people left destitute by the German occupation. Hoover and Wilbur both rose from modest means, and both attended Stanford because it then charged no tuition. Railroad baron Leland Stanford and his wife, Jane, wished this beneficence for the university they opened in 1891 as a memorial to their son on the 8,180-acre Palo Alto stock farm that became the campus. Yet the school struggled after the founders' deaths to sustain itself through railroad bonds and rentals of the agricultural lands that gave it the nickname "The Farm." Students from rich families paid no tuition while driving fancy cars and partying all over the state, and many of Wilbur's first moves upon assuming Stanford's presidency in 1916 aimed to crack down on what the era called "ornaments," or playboys, and impose the egalitarianism Hoover sought and the moral rigor Bourn championed.

From Hoover and his aides in Europe, Wilbur heard vivid accounts of wartime suffering that contrasted with the pastoral lassitude back home on The Farm. He learned of their helplessness at hearing distress calls "every half hour from ships that were being destroyed" by German submarines, knowing that "none of those calls could of course be answered" by their own unarmed ships. Sooner than many Americans—sooner, in fact, than Hoover himself—Wilbur became convinced that the United States must take up arms. Summoned by War Secretary Newton D. Baker to a gathering of college leaders on May 5, 1917, on how best "to disseminate correct information" about the war, he hotly protested the insufficiency of that charge and urged that universities take a far more activist role. "Coming here from California, where we seem to be much more awake than people think we are, I had expected here in Washington that we would at least find things moving...We have got to be willing to throw over some of our bureaucratic machinery and get right down to business."[12]

Wilbur was already planning what he and Stanford could do to get "things moving." Three weeks earlier, on April 18, the campus *Daily* had reported that he had directed his engineering faculty to mull "practical problems in connection with the theoretical encampment of a division of troops on a tract near the campus." This was the future Camp Fremont, though city leaders, Spring Valley and the university would spend months negotiating its borders. That this news first appeared thirty miles from the city whose

Stanford University president Ray Lyman Wilbur, *left*, fought image problems created by his antiwar predecessor David Starr Jordan, *right*. *Stanford University Archives.*

residents would be tapped to fund the camp would prove a costly lapse. Wilbur offered the land, he intimated later, for Stanford's sake as well as America's. The school had a "pacifistic reputation" that was proving very damaging, and he felt he had to live it down.[13]

Stanford's founding president, David Starr Jordan, was a renowned peace advocate who spent much of early 1917 barnstorming for neutrality. He was more famous and far more controversial than his immediate successor, John Casper Branner, who had merely griped to the *New York Times* that "the great difficulty about military instruction is that it leads either nowhere or to trouble" and confers only "an ability to do something that nobody wants done." The War Department's Commission on Training Camp Activities was soon to ban at least one of Jordan's books, 1914's *War and Waste*, in its drive to hone troops' patriotic edge.

As war fever deepened, Jordan's pacifism became a liability to the university. "Trustees and administrators could not shrug it off," wrote a contemporary, Stanford English instructor Edith Mirrielees. Fellow academics booed Stanford presenters off the podium at conferences and pilloried them in the press. Jordan's formal connection to the university had ended in 1916, but this fact was lost on the public. By March 1917, his East Coast speeches were met with near-riots. Princeton's president barred him from the podium there, while Cornell alumni sought to revoke his degree.

"It now seems clear that if we are to be a part in the future, we must take a man's part in the present," Wilbur countered in his March 1917 "Inescapable Responsibility" speech urging Stanford to do all it could for war: "Our duty is as plain as the fact that we have neglected it." On March 30, Stanford trustees voted to guarantee full salary for the looming war's duration of any staffer joining the war effort. On April 9, at a special meeting three days after Congress's war declaration, they sent the Associated Press a seven-point memo listing this and other patriotic efforts in answer to the "[m]any inquiries…received by authorities of Stanford University concerning its attitude toward war and the national preparation." They asserted that "[e]very element of Stanford—faculty, alumni, undergraduates and trustees—is united in support of…the active prosecution of the war." As Mirrielees remembered, "Few acquainted with the situation failed to understand the reason for there being a statement at all."[14]

Along with Hoover and many Stanford personnel, Wilbur joined the "dollar-a-year men" who powered the burgeoning wartime bureaucracy. He served first as Hoover's aide in the wartime Food Administration and later as an educational director for the War Department. This work kept him in

Washington for much of 1917 and 1918 and deferred many Camp Fremont problems to administrators acting in his stead, first biologist J.M. Stillman and then civil engineering professor Charles D. Marx. Marx was a centrist progressive of the type who drove the modernization of many U.S. cities, including Palo Alto, where he lived. A champion of publicly owned utilities and good government, he both designed and helped to manage much of Palo Alto's public works. Marx was called in to help design both Camp Fremont's water system and, eventually, the sewer system that the army built only partially and after much arm-twisting by California politicians. Marx's progressivism helps explain why he took on many additional duties in connection with the camp, only some of which were paid. In the progressive mindset, camps like Fremont were not merely chunks of political pork but powerful instruments for good. Just as they rolled out a carpet of infrastructure onto a rural landscape, the camps augured to blanket that same landscape with moral and social improvements: cleanliness, health, middle-class values. "You sometimes wonder why some of our home cities cannot be so ideally administered," a Menlo Park businessman wrote, somewhat optimistically, of Camp Fremont. "Maybe it was necessary for Uncle Sam to step in and first show them how to do it." There was much in prewar Menlo Park that progressives like Marx would have found in need of improving.[15]

Walter Hoag and his business partner, banker William Lansdale, bought and subdivided a great deal of what is now Menlo Park in 1907–8. The pair anticipated a rush of clients fleeing San Francisco after the 1906 earthquake and fire. Hoag marketed their subdivisions in a slick brochure featuring moody, picturesque photos of eucalyptus; the deep San Francisquito creek bed that bounded their Stanford Park subdivision on the east; and the massive oaks that, parklike indeed, dotted the land.

> *Menlo Park is a beautiful country, as yet untouched by the Boomer and Small Lot man...* [It] *possesses high class educational advantages, a complete Sanitary District...No other tract of land fronts on the University Grounds as does Stanford Park...It lies in fact nearer to the University buildings than Palo Alto...Sewer and water mains will be laid.*[16]

Hoag's sales pitch was, alas, a bit oversold. Stanford Park was separated from its "high class" namesake not only by city and county lines but also by a deep and wide creek bed that Hoag lacked permission to bridge. The local economy was tiny, notwithstanding the bustling, progressive university town of Palo Alto across the creek and Santa Clara County line. Menlo Park residents, unlike Palo Alto's, tended to be either part-timers from the city or the tradesmen and laborers who served them, plus the occasional proprietor of a roadhouse or "blind pig," an illegal liquor store. None but the affluent could hope to commute to San Francisco. The inexpensive streetcars that did so much to suburbanize other parts of the nation reached no farther than the town of San Mateo, ten miles north. Instead, locals rode the Southern Pacific rail line, pricey at $1.30 round trip to the city at a time when skilled tradesmen earned $4 to $6 a day. This was unfortunate for Hoag and his subdivisions, but probably a tremendous selling point for Camp Fremont and the army. It meant that Camp Fremont privates, paid $30 a month, could not afford to reach the brothels and bars of San Francisco. Every year, the ubiquity of the private automobile that would make Hoag's projects viable became nearer. But in 1917, it had not yet arrived.

That wasn't all. Hoag's lots were too small for the septic systems that handle waste in rural areas. State health authorities required them to have sewerage. Hoag began a sewer line in Stanford Park, but slow sales halted construction until Fitzpatrick and Rolph's committee came knocking on his door.

While Fitzpatrick and Rolph wrangled Menlo Park's other, mostly absentee, landowners, some of whom held out for higher rents, Rolph's committee sought army maneuver rights in Spring Valley's foothill watershed, and Rolph and U.S. Senator James D. Phelan of San Francisco lobbied the War Department. It probably helped that Phelan, a Democrat, was Woodrow Wilson's 1916 campaign chairman in California, which kept Wilson in the White House when he carried the state by a scant four thousand votes. After brief looks at Contra Costa County, Millbrae and a small town near Palo Alto called Mayfield, the government accepted the following offer:

> *San Francisco offers to procure for the War Department one year lease, rent free, on approximately 25,000 acres of land in the vicinity of Palo Alto, California...This property to be used by the War Department for Army training purposes for approximately a division of troops...Also agrees to cause a suitable water supply to be piped from the limits of the cantonment...Also to deliver sufficient gas and electrical...Also to provide ample outfall sewage line from limits of Camp.*
>
> *Respectfully, James Rolph, Jr.*
>
> *Mayor of the City and County of San Francisco*[17]

On July 6, the selection of Camp Fremont was made public. It was the last of the thirty-two camps to be announced. It was named after John C. Frémont, the army scout and adventurer who named the Golden Gate and claimed California for the United States in 1846. A portion of Santa Clara County south of the camp was surveyed in the nineteenth century as "Fremont Township," probably in honor of Frémont's mapping expeditions, and this as much as Frémont's romantic associations with Manifest Destiny may account for the camp's name. The Eighth Division formed at Camp Fremont was called the "Pathfinder Division" in tribute to Frémont, and this name stuck until the division's inactivation in 1992.

Peninsula lore holds that Mayfield lost out because of its many saloons, but the clause of the Selective Service Act that imposed a five-mile dry zone around military installations would have quickly shut them down. Nor were Menlo Park or San Mateo County especially virtuous. The lead story of the *Redwood City Democrat* on April 19, 1917, told of the conviction of a Menlo Park woman by an all-female jury (California women having won the vote in 1911) for running a "blind pig" for thirsty neighbors. Its lead story the day the army announced Camp Fremont was "Ordinance Will End Boxing Game in Redwood." More likely, the committee sited the camp in Menlo Park because, as de Young intimated a few months later, the land ultimately chosen was less costly and its owners more mindful of the benefits they thought a camp would bring.

On July 26, 1917, Stanford trustees moved to lease more than six thousand acres—more than three-quarters of the university's Palo Alto property, with a buffer around campus buildings—for use by the War Department for $40,000 a year. Although this sum was to be guaranteed to Stanford by the citizens' committee, the committee had trouble raising the funds, and the fee was soon reduced to $25,000. The government paid to build the actual camp. The owners of the land leased "rent free" were actually to be compensated and their property taxes paid, if desired, by public donations to the committee led by Rolph and managed by San Francisco city clerk J.S. Dunnigan and Britton of PG&E. Camp contracts were overseen by a triumvirate that included Hoag & Lansdale associate George Burlingame and Rolph's brother George, a sugar company executive. The committee pledged to raise $150,000 for the land leases and other expenses, including $55,000 for a sewer outfall from the camp to the bay.

The army accepted the bid as written but planned no sewer system. Fremont was to be a National Guard camp and, as such, was planned for only brief occupation. No civilian, including Hoag, seems to have understood

Stateside troops ate plentifully, while civilians "Hooverized," or conserved, to save food for the fighting men and for Allied food relief. *Menlo Park Historical Association.*

what this might mean. They were educated days after the bid was granted, when state officials moved to block Camp Fremont's construction as a threat to public health. Stanford trustee Timothy Hopkins wired Phelan, urging his personal intervention: "Latrines out of the question in thickly populated district with a porous soil from which water supply is pumped... You are familiar with the locality and the community and myself personally would appreciate your seeing Secretary Baker that proper instructions may be issued to prevent danger of contamination of the soil." Perhaps not coincidentally, the army's original plan called for waste from camp kitchens and showers to drain into San Francisquito Creek, bordering Hopkins's Menlo Park property downstream. Stanford threatened to back out of its lease, thereby jeopardizing the entire camp. Hopkins knew the community's drainage problems well, for he was a member of the local sanitary board.[18]

Phelan went straight to War Secretary Baker, and federal money was duly promised for Camp Fremont sewerage. Marx, already one of three men tapped to design the camp's water system, took on the sewerage as well. The robust clay-pipe system Marx designed for Camp Fremont linked existing lines to the northwest, in what is now Atherton, with Hoag's Stanford Park subdivision to the southeast. The money that the War Department found proved enough to build this main line through what is now downtown Menlo Park and to link it to Rolph's outfall but stopped short of extending the system to all but about 15 percent of the camp. Units graced with flush toilets included camp headquarters and Fremont's corps of engineers regiment, which helped Marx lay out the system. One line, later dubbed the "Army Line," served Menlo Park until the twenty-first century. The rest of Camp Fremont's troops used hand-dug privies, even if a sewer line ran a few yards away. By 1927, numerous small-lot subdivisions had sprung up along the sewer outfall to the bay.

It is not easy now to tease out the love of country from the love of gain that motivated civic boosters who agreed to host the camp. Doubtless it was not easy then. Hoag's motivation is revealed in his fury after the war when he learned that the U.S. Public Health Service planned to keep the land he had provided for the base hospital, complete with brand-new sewer underneath. "This lease was in no sense a profitable lease," he fumed. The $124,000 that Hoag's National Land Company later got from the government probably softened his ire. Much of the sixty-eight thousand acres that Rolph eventually obtained from a patchwork of Peninsula landowners was never used except as drill grounds or woodlots, the camp's appetite for firewood being insatiable. It did include twenty-five thousand acres around both termini of today's Dumbarton Bridge, not far from the army engineers' 1910 rail bridge. Its inclusion might have facilitated army construction of the auto bridge, not to mention development nearby, had the land not reverted at war's end to its private owners, the Dumbarton Land and Improvement Company.[19]

Still, it is illogical and ahistorical to criticize self-interest in a war mobilization that relied on self-interest. Until mid-1918, when Congress passed laws to expedite eviction and condemnation proceedings in service of war aims, the government had no way to acquire the vast tracts of land required, with the speed required, except by appeal to whatever motivation spurred their owners' giving. It didn't always work to lean blatantly on self-interest, as Rolph's committee found while trying to raise Camp Fremont funds from a skeptical public. Better to allow donors to project generosity and self-sacrifice, to appeal to their altruism rather than their need. A piece in the *Stanford Illustrated Review* deftly unwinds the entwined lures of patriotism and profit that Camp Fremont offered: "Owners of land near the camp began to look up the new automobile numbers" while praising themselves for welcoming "the Great Adventure" to their doors. The piece is headlined "Fremont, the Flirt."[20]

Stanford, for its part, needed the money as well as the patriotic rehabilitation that Camp Fremont so seductively offered. Though Stanford's endowment surpassed $20 million, most of it was in railroad bonds, some of which failed to pay dividends during the labor unrest of the war years, and in far-flung ranchland difficult to monetize. The university had $162,897 cash on hand at the end of fiscal 1917–18; its faculty payroll averaged $47,000 a month. In that fiscal year, the $25,000 that Stanford ultimately received for Camp Fremont was equivalent to the total allocation for the university library. In short, the $25,000 Stanford got for leasing its grounds was hardly game-changing, but it was a helpful boost until trustees could create other income streams.

The lease money dribbled in to the citizens' committee slowly, however, sometimes in gifts of a single dollar. It took a surprising nine months for Rolph's committee to raise the money it had pledged. In the end, it ran $11,000 short of the $150,000 promised. During these months, Camp Fremont construction proceeded in fits and starts. Its unionized building

A placard given to donors to the fund that paid Stanford and others who leased land for the camp. *Political Poster Collection, US 5027, Hoover Institution Archives. Courtesy of Hoover Institution Library & Archives, Stanford University.*

workers walked out at least twice. The army sent its first wave of western draftees to other camps, principally Lewis and Kearny.

Britton, the PG&E executive whom Rolph tapped as Camp Fremont's fundraising chairman, began by targeting San Francisco businessmen. He broke them down by industry sector and asked one hundred men each to raise $1,500 from fellow grocers, clothiers and so on. He told these San Franciscans they would prosper from additional business from the camp—"nearly $1 million in each monthly payroll," he claimed. It was only fair for the middle class to contribute, Britton intimated, since not just the rich would benefit from the camp's presence. Donors to the "Camp Fremont Fund" received a colorful placard featuring John C. Frémont to put in their windows. Britton spent little time soliciting people in San Mateo and Santa Clara Counties, where the camp was located. He said it was because comparatively few people lived there. Still, Peninsula voters' growing fear of amalgamation and of being asked to shoulder the city's bonded indebtedness probably played a role. Britton told the *Chronicle*, "The business interests of San Francisco should recognize the importance of the mobilization of 20,000 or more men in our immediate neighborhood...We can surely afford to put up $150,000 to secure an expenditure of $2,250,000 a month by the Government. The people of San Francisco should make good on their promises and obligations."[21]

Britton's appeals bombed. By Thanksgiving 1917, he had raised only one-tenth of the $150,000 promised. Some people made pledges but failed to pay after seeing camp construction repeatedly shut down. The army moved the Forty-first National Guard, troops from the Pacific Northwest who were the camp's initial occupants, to Camp Greene in Charlotte, North Carolina, amid one such closure. Army Major General Arthur Murray told Rolph he wanted to see $100,000 in earnest money by mid-December or the camp would close for good. "Washington keeps asking us where the money is," Lieutenant Colonel Richard Park, acting chief of staff, told the *Chronicle*. The general contracting firm of Lindgren & Co. was the largest creditor, being owed $55,000 for the sewer outfall to the bay that it had begun over the summer. Stanford was second in line. Not until April 1918 were all Camp Fremont's leases settled.[22]

The delay is puzzling, as is Britton's strategy, considering that almost everyone on Rolph's committee was rich—many of them rich enough to cover the pledge personally, were they so inclined. Some, like Britton of PG&E and Eastman of Spring Valley, were Camp Fremont vendors who by late 1917 had already sunk infrastructure into the camp and had motive to see it through. They lived, furthermore, in a prosperous city that prided itself on generosity in time of crisis, that called itself since rebuilding after the 1906 disaster "The City that Knows How." Within a few months in 1917, San Franciscans raised $1 million for the Red Cross and subscribed for $51 million to the Second Liberty Loan. A *Chronicle* editorial pleaded donor fatigue as San Franciscans, like other Americans, were hounded by pleas

The government initially aimed at men's nobler instincts. Rather than wait to be drafted, some men enlisted to choose their branch of service. *National Archives.*

on behalf of more Liberty Bond issues, War Savings Stamps, Red Cross missions and so on, often with civic quotas that rose with each campaign.

The mayor's daybooks show he kept himself involved. He labeled one August 22 meeting "Dunnigan and Hoag lunched my home re: Camp Fremont troubles" and another "Meeting re: Camp Fremont mess." Moreover, he endorsed Britton's tactics, telling constituents that "it will all come back to the merchants of San Francisco, a million and a half a month. You never had a better opportunity." Instead, contemporary documents show that Camp Fremont neared its fundraising target only when its strategists ceased to invoke self-interest—ironically, the very motivation that commended the camp to many of its hosts in the first place—and switched to the loftier rhetoric of philanthropy and self-sacrifice that other public appeals used successfully.[23]

Labor strife during camp construction probably hurt the cause. It would have alarmed union partisans and spooked others. San Francisco's strong union heritage meant that its middle class often followed labor's cues rather than capital's in forming its opinions, according to historian Michael Kazin. The National Guard had trouble recruiting in San Francisco because the militia was so often used to break strikes. Unlike the American Federation of Labor's Samuel Gompers, who rationalized the war as an engine of social progress and joined Wilson's advisory team in 1916, San Francisco's Building Trades Council delayed public support of the war until months after the United States entered it. On July 24, 1917, the Forty-first National Guard newly arrived at Camp Fremont was sent to break a strike by cannery workers in San Jose, prompting San Francisco labor to rally in support. The camp's union plumbers and electricians themselves soon struck for higher wages, but a greater dispute was over commute costs, which many workers found so onerous that they failed to show up at all. Lindgren wound up appealing to the government to cover workers' train fare, $25,000 of which it was still trying to collect after the Armistice. Moreover, the army paid union wages but, unlike nearly all San Francisco workplaces, kept an open shop. Camp Fremont's constructing quartermaster claimed the camp's union workers harassed the nonunion ones so badly that he had to segregate union and nonunion crews.

On a practical level, the San Francisco merchants whom Rolph and Britton solicited may simply not have agreed that they were in a position to profit from an army base thirty miles away. Military procurement opportunities already abounded in the city, many of them advertised weekly in the *San Francisco Chamber of Commerce Activities.* As it happened, many of

Camp Fremont's smaller orders, such as for office supplies and light bulbs, were eventually filled by local firms in Palo Alto. The concept of a "Greater San Francisco" did not resonate with the city's middle class as it did the oligarchy, just as it was encountering resistance among suburban voters. San Franciscans did not agree that they were implicated in a "civic pledge," in the *Chronicle*'s words, involving land so far away. Oddly, Britton's appeals do not mention the "soldier boys" at all, only their payroll statistics. This was the wrong tack to take in the provisioning of a citizen army whose members came from prospective donors' own families.

More ominously, San Franciscans did not like that the citizens' committee met behind closed doors and produced the camp as a *fait accompli* that it then asked the public to fund. Residents had grown used to public debate over civic issues, notably such touchstone progressive issues as public ownership of city streetcar lines and water supply. Rolph's white-glove committee, meeting in secrecy, did not align with his vow to be "mayor of all the people." There was, one infers from statements made by Rolph and de Young in October, objection raised that the "promises and obligations" had not in fact been made by "the people of San Francisco," but by a few business titans in a closed room. De Young tried to explain:

> *No account of this meeting was published, as we thought it bad policy to publish it to the world that we were likely to get a camp here...There were different holders of large acreage who did not want to give up their land to the government...We did not want a fight on our hands...So city authorities went ahead, and with others there assured the holders of the land that the people of San Francisco would come through and make good our promises...We probably made a mistake in not taking the people into our confidence before...You can raise this amount in three or four days.*[24]

De Young's reference to "holders of large acreage" probably refers to Spring Valley, which was initially reported to be offering the camp large tracts in the foothills but backpedaled before the deal was finalized. While Spring Valley, along with dozens of Peninsula landowners, did later volunteer land toward the sixty-thousand-plus-acre military reservation associated with the camp, it also cited the temporary spike in consumption represented by its Camp Fremont water contract to begin residential water metering and permanently raise rates for its customers in San Francisco. De Young's admission that his group's secrecy hid spatting over such issues would only have further alienated the public.

Growing war zeal led to a harder sell. Harry Hopps's poster exemplifies America's demonization of the Central Powers. *Library of Congress.*

In truth, his committee's strategy failed to offer most San Franciscans a reason to support the camp. They united against common threats such as the 1906 earthquake. The distant war had to be phrased in the terms used by George Creel of the Committee on Public Information: as a common threat to all Americans. Instead, the committee's strategy to raise funds for Camp Fremont exposed the cleavages that crisscrossed wartime America rather than dissolving them.

At the eleventh hour, a *Chronicle* writer, Helen Dare, struck the note that Britton and Rolph had failed to ring:

> *Listen, friends! And this means you—everyone that takes pride in or has interests in this home town of ours. San Francisco's...record for generosity, her perfectly justified contention that she's not a piker—all, ALL are at stake this minute...Don't, for want of initiative, for want of pep, for want of real pride in your city...stand back until it is too late and lose the race in the home stretch.*
>
> *From the sentimental point of view, it matters to the mothers and sweethearts and sisters, to the fathers and brothers and uncles, too, of the soldier boys to have them in training here at home as long as possible, instead of way off somewhere where they'll be lonesome...Don't leave it all for the capitalists to do, don't stand from under and say it's up to the rich fellows to pull it through, for it means as much to the little fellows in business and to those who are interested merely through sentiment...as it* [does] *to the captains of Big Business to have a great soldier camp at our door.*[25]

Simply put, Americans responded when their generosity, rather than their need, was appealed to. This insight was one that Creel would mine in his "advertising"—his word—of the war.

It seems odd today to think of the U.S. military as a charity to be funded through individual giving. Yet that is precisely what the war effort did. The Liberty Loans, though they drew huge institutional buyers, were advertised as a way everyday Americans could help their country in time of need. The Camp Fremont fundraising campaign, though on a much smaller scale, worked when it, too, intimated that America, as an entity, was in need of charitable assistance. This aid could come from the "little fellows" as well as "the capitalists." The appeal derived from the progressive sentiment that the country had something wrong with it that needed fixing—a "drift" away from shared purpose. Giving was a way of joining the cause. It was a way of contributing to the remedy, of funding an army that would fix America's problems as well as the world's. Rolph and Britton were both veteran fundraisers, but they did not grasp this new and powerful paradigm. Creel and his Committee on Public Information used it to amass the enormous funds needed to mobilize for war.

Dare's appeal ran on the *Chronicle*'s women's page, where it appears to have been read by both genders. The *Chronicle* noted on December 25 that the fund had taken in $2,615 since the Saturday prior, for a total of $114,640. This was enough to show the army "earnest money," and Camp Fremont was saved.

Chapter 2

TRENCH AND CAMPUS

Stanford Rallies Around the Flag

As 1918 opened, Camp Fremont sputtered to life. Regular Army infantry units marched south in January from the Presidio of San Francisco, a three-day hike with bivouacs at Colma and San Mateo, to replace the departed 41st National Guard. These infantry ranks were soon augmented by draftees transferred from other camps. Other units formed at Fremont largely from California volunteers, including the 319th Engineers and the base hospital staff. In February, Brigadier General Joseph D. Leitch took interim command, followed by Major General John F. Morrison on March 10. They were the first generals to do so; their predecessors had been colonels supervising other colonels, and not much got done. The camp was still only partly built when Leitch arrived, with few roads, little hot water and no mess halls, so that scruffy men ate outside in the wintry chill. It was far from the model city cheerfully described by journalist Ida Tarbell and other progressive observers of the nation's training camps. Yet with commanders with stars on their shoulders, Camp Fremont's pace began to quicken, and the camp began to fill and to grow.

Among Leitch's and Morrison's objectives was the acquisition of the full twenty-five thousand acres that Rolph's citizens' committee in San Francisco had promised the army in its bid for the camp. In addition to more land for maneuvers and drill, Leitch and Morrison wanted Camp Fremont to have an artillery range. Rolph's committee had procured about seven thousand acres, most of it Stanford's, before running out of money. If the army wanted more land as things stood in early 1918, it

A low-flying aerial photographer captures Camp Fremont at mess. Troops arrived long before buildings were complete. *Stanford University Archives.*

had to persuade camp-adjacent owners to provide it gratis. If it wanted to use land already acquired, including Stanford's, in ways more intensive or destructive than the maneuvers and drill that the leases allowed, it was obliged to seek occupants' consent. Refusals were few in a climate of public opinion that lauded the war effort. In the case of the artillery program, however, some people did resist.

The carving of Camp Fremont's artillery range and the quarters for its artillerymen from reluctant occupants' lands over many months in 1917–18 tells in microcosm the tale of America's war mobilization. It reveals the haphazard nature of a mobilization begun largely through voluntary efforts. It reveals the government's shift from persuasion to coercion as Congress enacted laws in the spring of 1918 that gave the executive branch sweeping wartime powers, including, as eventually happened at Stanford, the ability to take land and evict tenants without judicial consent. It reveals the growing war zeal that fostered these laws despite their evident unconstitutionality. Because building the U.S. artillery was an important goal, it offers a relatively palatable argument for such laws. Though the army realized soon after entering the war that it had to greatly expand its artillery strength, it spent nearly a year getting these units formed, housed, equipped and trained. Camp Fremont's artillery saga exemplifies the delays that military historians say hindered AEF performance and contributed to heavy casualties.

Meanwhile, the camp nibbled away at more than land. It encroached on Stanford classes and programs and on the thoughts and lives of people living nearby as Americans were obliged with increasing stridency not just to "do their bit" but sacrificially to "do their best."

The first troops of Camp Fremont's Eighth Artillery Brigade arrived on Valentine's Day 1918, occupying two hundred acres of Stanford land bounded by Governor's Avenue and San Francisquito Creek that a Stanford tenant, one M.H. Tichenor, had subleased to the army the summer before. The gunners' proximity to campus women disturbed many civilians in that more genteel age and revived a public-relations problem that Stanford would rather have put to rest. Back in July 1917, the army had reneged on its agreement to use Stanford land for maneuvers and drill rather than for soldiers' quarters, which the university understood would be across the creek in Menlo Park. It sought the Tichenor acres, roughly a quarter of a mile from Stanford's women's dormitory and gym, to quarter one of the artillery units that the army was then beginning to add to divisional organizations. Tichenor ran a dairy on the property for San Francisco capitalist Herbert Fleishhacker, who was active in the committee that brought Camp Fremont to the Bay Area. It is possible that Fleishhacker or Tichenor discussed the sublease with the army before informing Stanford and that this omission contributed to Stanford's surprise. General Hunter Liggett reassured the university that "no soldiers will be permitted to pass the lines formed by the fences on the road sides bounding this ground and nearest the University grounds" and that "every possible precaution" would be taken to respect campus life. Trustees seethed, but they told their lawyers to draw up the paperwork.[26]

Governor's Avenue gave onto a throughway to the central part of campus that offered troops a beeline to whatever Stanford amenities, including female students, they wished to pursue. Charles D. Marx, who acted in Wilbur's stead during his many war-related absences and to whom many Camp Fremont problems thus devolved, spent months wrangling with the army about whether Governor's Avenue was included in the lease and whether troops had the right to use it. The flap over the Tichenor sublease made headlines and created a dilemma for the university. On one hand, it threatened to revive the image Wilbur was trying to kill of Stanford as anti-war and thus anti-American. On the other, it made outlets like the *Argonaut*, a once-sparkling San Francisco journal grown reactionary with age, fear for Stanford's very soul: "In the countries which have now been at war for nearly three years conditions like that about to be created at Palo Alto have resulted

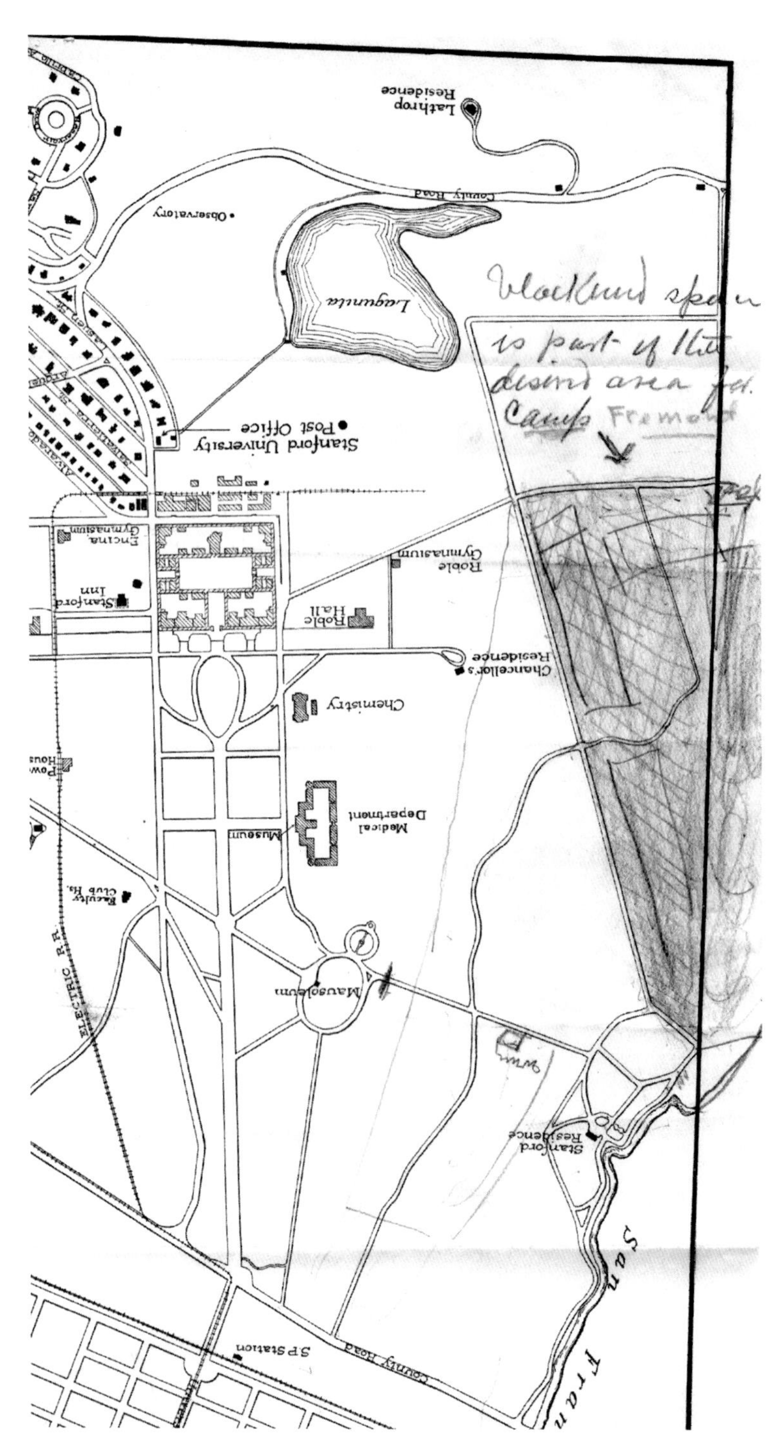

Professor J.M. Stillman complained to Wilbur in July 1917 about the army's plan to put troops less than five hundred yards from the women's dormitory. *Stanford University Archives.*

Camp Fremont sentry duty was a prized detail and a permeable barrier, as this cartoon by a Twelfth Infantry man points out. *From* The Twelfth U.S. Infantry—Its Story by Its Men.

in wholesale breakdown of moral restraints…We have here the suggestion of a problem both delicate and difficult that the authorities of the university must look frankly in the face."[27]

Marx's predecessor, J.M. Stillman, perhaps made bold by his imminent retirement, was quoted in the papers as opposing this use of Stanford land for soldiers' quarters. "Having the camp approach any nearer than necessary to the buildings and athletic grounds of the women," he wrote to Wilbur, "limits, to some extent, their freedom." Wilbur scolded him from Washington, calling his remarks "gratuitous, to say the least." To Marx, Wilbur telegraphed: "Understand from night letter…that there are rumors about Stanford objecting to army encampment. Certainly there can be no idea of keeping soldiers off from the campus…Hope this agrees your ideas, [board president W. Mayo] Newhall's. Athletic contests between soldiers and students desirable."[28]

The army detailed two companies—about three hundred men—to patrol the contested border. It was a prized detail, according to one winking newspaper story, and a permeable barrier, as it turned out. Stanford, for its part, opened its sports facilities to the soldiers, then placed its female students in virtual lockdown after dark to "protect" them until after the end of the war.

It might be fair to call Wilbur, as the *Argonaut* later did, "authoritarian and absentee," yet his writings indicate that he had at heart not only the Allies' interests but also Stanford's in pushing the university's militarization. Still, the Tichenor flap and Wilbur's role in it established the institutional tensions that would characterize Stanford's relations with Camp Fremont through the Armistice. As the army's needs expanded, it reinterpreted in its own favor its original, often nebulous and poorly drafted, agreements with the university. Wilbur urged acquiescence for the sake of public opinion and Stanford pride. The price of the university's unsullied image, in other words, was material encroachment.[29]

Thus went a war effort dependent on voluntarism and self-interest, dependent, as the Committee on Public Information's George Creel wrote, "not wholly [on] the strength of the arm of the soldier…but rather the mental forces that were at work nerving those arms." By fits and starts, Stanford ended up hosting not only the Eighth Artillery Brigade but also the range on which it practiced, as well as other weapons ranges including a trench maneuver ground. A San Francisco businessman running one of the city chamber of commerce's endless appeals for war funds, this time for War Savings Stamps, in April 1918 voiced the stress-inducing note with which all wartime Americans, like Stanford, were asked to part with their possessions and time: "Are you doing your bit or doing your best?…Every one of us here is in this war, and *must* sacrifice at the nation's call everything that the country calls upon him to sacrifice." A large initial response, such as Stanford's lease of its grounds, did not let the donor off the hook but rather enlisted him to do more.[30]

The land that Camp Fremont sought for its artillery range included a one-thousand-foot hill for firing positions behind the university and several miles of hilly grassland and forest beyond that made it ideal for targets. It forms the backdrop to Stanford Memorial Church in iconic images of the campus. Some of it, including the firing positions on Dish Hill, was in the original six thousand acres leased in 1917 from Stanford. The rest was among sixty-thousand-plus acres secured without compensation by the army from Stanford and other landowners in early 1918 for potential maneuvers, woodlots and drill. Highways in the vicinity, including Alpine and Arastradero roads, were blocked during the bombardments, and this, too, was laid to wartime sacrifice. Thirteen landowners and six tenants were obliged to clear their land of people and livestock.

One of these owners was Richard M. Hotaling, whose 738 acres of cattle range on either side of Arastradero abutted Stanford lands. Hotaling had reasons to believe in his exceptionalism. He and his brother, Anson Jr., ran the family's large liquor distributorship in San

Map detail of Camp Fremont's artillery range. Then mostly cattle pasture, today it is largely restricted-use open space. The serpentine line is Arastradero Road. *National Archives.*

Francisco. Their warehouse, with contents, survived the 1906 earthquake and fire while thousands of structures burned, thanks to firefighters and employees who went to heroic efforts to save it. The Hotaling blood ran to "extreme latitudinarianism," in one biographer's view, and another writer, Richard's Bohemian Club buddy Charles Kellogg Field, saw a perverse Providence at work:

> *If, as they say, God spanked the town*
> *For being over frisky,*
> *Why did He burn the churches down*
> *And save Hotaling's whiskey?*[31]

On February 19, 1918, Hotaling very politely declined the army's request that he vacate his land for Camp Fremont target practice. His letter illustrates

Richard Hotaling's nonconformist views extended to his highly qualified support of America's war mobilization. *Bancroft Library, University of California–Berkeley.*

several points of disconnect between popular conceptions of war in 1918 and the actuality:

> *This morning I was called upon by High Private Abrahams...He told me...that a wild shot or glancing bullet might do injury to livestock or persons that The Hotaling Estate Company have by permit granted the troops of the United States Army the privilege of access for military maneuvering...The lands are more than three miles away from the location of the targets. Between these targets and these lands there are two series of low rolling hills... It is extremely unlikely that any danger whatever will result...*
>
> *Because of the intervening hills.*
>
> *Because of the distance...*
>
> *To interfere in any way with agricultural conditions...*[requires first that] *every effort be made to avoid doing so. The cry that has gone up "Food Will Win the War" should receive every possible observance that the Food Administration is calling to it...*
>
> [T]*he demands for military conditions should be enforced in such way that civilians will not look upon any condition in this country as being akin to the spirit that we are now fighting and which is so viciously demonstrated in the militarism of Germany.*

Hotaling in sum, refused to evict his tenants. He informed the army that if the army itself did so, he expected the government not only to indemnify the tenants for their cost of moving but also to cover his own lost rent.[32]

Hotaling's declaration of independence was brave at the time and probably unusual. Under the wartime Espionage and Sedition Acts, publications were shut down and people jailed for less. Over the county line in Hillsborough, a San Mateo County judge jailed a Boer War veteran for five days for impugning the U.S. flag. The *Redwood City Tribune* reported in mid-May 1917 that more than one hundred other Bay Area residents, mostly immigrants, had been jailed or fined for disloyalty since the April 6 war declaration. Before the Espionage Act's enactment in June, such personal dissents were prosecuted as violations of Wilson's curbs on enemy aliens, proclaimed the day that Congress voted to declare war, or, in the case of U.S. citizens, as conspiracy to obstruct the Selective Service Act. While spies and labor radicals were undeniably the main targets, zealous misinterpretations reveal how tense the times were. The mayor of Oakland vowed soon after Wilson's April 6 proclamation to lock up any residents who failed to display the U.S. flag. Sonoma County deputies arrested a fifteen-year-old boy and his Swiss-born father for operating a radio set on their isolated farm.

What is made clear by all such reports, certainly, is a chilling atmosphere of repression that was amplified in the popular press. The era's great apologist for democracy, Senator Hiram Johnson, famously expressed sentiments similar to Hotaling's that surely must have been shared by others despite statutory repression and self-censorship. "The fact is," Johnson wrote a friend in 1918, "we are no longer a Republic... [T]he design of the Government has been

Troops were taught to dig and maintain trenches. These are student cadets awaiting induction, but inductees logged hours of similar drill. *Stanford University Archives.*

in this war to repress, suppress, and to hold a people, deprived of all those things which made for liberty of speech and action, wholly in subjection." Johnson could claim the shield of senatorial privilege, while Hotaling was on his own. The whiskey man was not alone in wanting to control army use of his land, however. At least two Stanford tenants refused to quit the artillery range even after bombardments had begun.[33]

Equally striking is the disconnect between Hotaling's idea of what the land would be used for and its eventual purpose. His letter betrays his assumption, evidently uncorrected by Private First Class Abrahams, that his land would be used for rifle practice, not for the far more destructive seventy-five-millimeter and six-inch field guns that would soon be aimed there. The land's distance from the gun positions, and the fact that hills lay between gun and target, were, far from being detrimental to the army's purpose, exactly what it was seeking to simulate battlefield topography on the Western Front. The "big guns" of the Great War were fired at great distance on unseen targets, using trigonometry to calculate firing positions. The average range of a seventy-five-millimeter field gun, smallest of the common artillery pieces, when firing shrapnel-filled shells was 3.6 miles. Often, gunners fired into reverse slopes like those in Hotaling's Palo Alto pastures to destroy enemy machine gun nests or artillery batteries concealed behind the hills.

Learning to land precise fire on distant positions was critical because of the great importance World War I artillery assumed in combination with infantry movement. Along with the trenches, a distinguishing feature of Western Front battle was the "creeping barrage" of successive artillery salvos that covered men moving from their trenches toward an enemy position. Army historian Richard Faulkner notes that few U.S. troops received much artillery training before sailing across the Atlantic. In part this was due to delays in acquiring munitions, which had to be calibrated to the Allies' metric scale. In part, Faulkner writes, it stemmed from generals' reluctance to follow Allied experts in an extreme application of General Pershing's wish for U.S. military autonomy. Some camps had no artillery until well into 1918, so that even those occupied sooner than late-blooming Fremont remained at a disadvantage. At Camp Pike in Arkansas, artillerymen executed maneuvers with logs mounted on caissons to simulate field weapons. Other camps had weapons but lacked suitable land.

Lack of training, Faulkner asserts, contributed to the AEF's problems in obtaining artillery-infantry coordination and thus to high casualties in its great fall 1918 offensives at St. Mihiel and the Meuse-Argonne. Of the mayhem that resulted when a covering barrage was not accurate, no tale may be more anguished than that of the "Hello Girl," or civilian phone operator in France, who mishandled a call from an AEF commander trying to cancel a barrage that was falling on his men. If, on the other hand, the barrage failed to materialize, the troops under Pershing's doctrine of "self-reliant infantry" still had to go over the top.

Few people outside the army knew anything about this, however, and Hotaling exemplified the common U.S. ignorance of the industrial warfare that the nation was preparing to join. He conceived of war, or at least war training, as many in his time did, as an essentially pastoral enterprise involving small arms and lots of health-building drill and marching through the countryside. Many in the preparedness movement cited this outdoor health-building aspect as a benefit of war training, and it entwined with a nostalgia that many progressives in the war effort harbored for America's pastoral past. "Romance is not wanting to-day when sunset finds an American field battery pushing across a trackless desert," *Collier's* sighed in one layout of hopelessly anachronistic training photos in April 1917, while a San Francisco retailer fretted that employees who had "lived the outdoor life of the soldier" would disdain their old jobs in his store.[34]

Since at least 1914, Stanford itself had leased maneuver rights over its foothills to U.S. cavalry units moving from the Presidio of Monterey to points north, an easy income stream compatible with the lands' agricultural tax status that may have lulled university officials into thinking Camp Fremont would be similar but on a larger scale. Maps and facts pertinent to actual warfare were kept secret for security reasons and unavailable to civilians. Thoughtful Americans could infer the terrible actuality new to the Great War—the death that rained unseen and unheralded from above, the obliteration of landscape—from the rare French or Canadian photos of the ravaged Western Front that crept past the Committee on Public Information into mass media such as *Collier's*. The war Americans were being told to support and to fund and to fight was inconceivable to most unless they were there.

The army appears to have done nothing to correct Hotaling's misconceptions. Declassified documents dating from the beginning of February 1918 never refer to the thirteen parcels sought in the foothills as anything but an artillery range. It is thus designated on a map surveyed and drawn in May 1918 by the 319th Engineers. Nor was Hotaling being totally disingenuous in citing the War Department's mandate on food production as an excuse to keep his ranching tenants on the land. The cry that "food will win the war" rang out not only from local son Herbert Hoover, whose leadership in the war effort was giving Stanford and indeed all of California

In a foreshadowing of World War II's victory gardens, the War Department urged Americans to grow food for home consumption. *Menlo Park Historical Association.*

new cachet, but ubiquitously from the CPI's publicity machine. Creel's agency urged Americans to "Intrench your homes with crops! Every bushel of corn or potatoes raised this season brings victory one hour nearer," for "to farm is as necessary as to arm."[35]

During the negotiations for the artillery range, in fact, the army itself sought Camp Fremont land on which to train soldiers to grow food. Having heard of the state's agricultural bounty, and wishing to keep troops busy while awaiting deployment, the army adjutant general in Washington dispatched a University of California agriculture expert to evaluate likely croplands at Fremont and at Camp Kearny, outside San Diego. Stanford protested this use of its land when it became clear that the army would not pay additional rentals and pointed out that the dry Mediterranean climate made most crops impossible without irrigation, which most of Stanford's rangeland lacked. San Francisco city clerk Dunnigan told the army, inaccurately but helpfully from Stanford's point of view, that all Camp Fremont's best agricultural land was located within the proposed artillery range, and the army let the matter drop.

Yet finally, and surprisingly, in April 1918, Camp Fremont's adjutant agreed to Hotaling's terms. The whiskey man's chief tenant, M.J. Borges, was "to be given notice by the leaving of a written notice at his ranch house at least 12 hours preceding the times when the lands are to be used by the government for artillery fire practice," the *Trench and Camp* newspaper reported. Forms for this purpose were duly drafted and sent to the commander of the Eighty-first Field Artillery for posting. Like their comrades in Fremont's two other artillery regiments, the camp's adjutant explained, the Eighty-first was getting impatient and had "not had any actual practice since coming here." On April 29, 1918, two days after the range leases were finally settled, a *Redwood City Tribune* writer rejoiced at the sound of the big guns firing beyond barricaded Alpine Road:

> *Battery E of the 81st Field Artillery and Battery D of the 83rd Field Artillery engaged an imaginary foe across the green swales and oak-covered hills in the neighborhood of the Drexel orphanage on the Menlo Park highway...The sight in these days of war was a most inspiring one to the civilians in the fact that real shells were used and that in the bursting of these there could be pictured in a miniature way the destruction that is being wrought on the battle-whipped plains of Picardy and in those sectors where the gallant Liberty Boys are so courageously holding their own. Words cannot explain adequately the picture of pastoral serenity, the deafening roar of the three-inch American type of gun, the wild bowl of the projectile, the far-off explosion and the accompanying geyser of dirt and debris rising into the air.*[36]

The guns tearing up this Elysium were the "French 75s" whose shells still occasionally surface in the Palo Alto foothills. At least one larger piece, a 155-millimeter or six-inch howitzer depending on the source, joined Camp Fremont's arsenal on June 1. This was both the apogee and the beginning of the end of Camp Fremont's artillery program, because the howitzer exploded on its maiden firing, instantly killing Private Henry Kuzio of the Second Field Artillery and mortally wounding a second artilleryman who died in Camp Fremont's hospital. Four more artillerymen were badly injured. Orders came that month to move all of Camp Fremont's gunners to Fort Sill, Oklahoma, where they arrived on June 30, finished their training and rejoined the rest of the Eighth Division only at its Atlantic point of embarkation. Unlike most Camp Fremont troops, the gunners made it to France, albeit too late to fight, as did a single Fremont infantry regiment, the Eighth.

As Camp Fremont fought for its artillery program, two relevant developments transpired elsewhere. Within a short time in the spring and early summer of 1918, Congress enacted several laws that broadly expanded executive power to further the war effort. Lawmakers acknowledged these laws' curbs on liberty but believed them necessary to speed what was proving to be a balky mobilization. Shock swept the nation, for example, when Americans learned that in the nation's much-touted aviation program, only a single airplane had left the production line. The executives and bureaucrats responsible proffered a circular firing squad of blame. Laws passed in response included the Overman, or Departmental Reorganization, Act (40 Stat. 556, May 20, 1918), which gave President Wilson the power to create and alter federal agencies and, conversely, broadened agencies' ability to act outside their mission fields. Enacted the same day as the Sedition Act, with its tightened curbs on war dissent, the lesser-known Housing for War Needs Act (40 Stat. 552, May 16, 1918) allowed government agencies to take land via eminent domain without going to court.

"Speed, speed, speed, is what is needed in this matter," explained Senator Claude Swanson of Virginia on the need to jettison what he termed the "cumbersome" process of judicial procedure. The Labor Department sought this law to assuage war-worker housing shortages, primarily at East Coast shipyards and in Washington, but it was written broadly enough to cover land sought for any wartime purpose. In tandem, the Overman and housing laws allowed almost any federal employee to claim almost any land in America in the government's name. Senator Hiram Johnson, aghast, explained the bills' upshot to a wealthy friend. "'Good God,' he said, 'if you pass such a law we might just as well be in Prussia.' I said, 'Keep still, because if we adopt the conference report [on the Sedition Act, enacted the same day] now before us, and you should make such a remark as that, 20 years will be your portion,' and under this bill that would be so."[37]

Artillerymen pose with seventy-five-millimeter field guns in the vicinity of the Stanford property now called Dish Hill. *Portola Valley Historical Association.*

Camp Fremont's adjutant general served the recalcitrant Stanford tenants a three-day eviction notice on May 21, 1918, one day after the Overman bill and five days after the housing bill became law. Stanford does not appear to have been of much help in the eviction, inasmuch as the adjutant was not supplied with the tenants' full names, information that certainly would have been in the university's files.

Yet both the evictions and the wrangles with Hotaling were pointless in the end. While Camp Fremont battled ranchers and traffic for its artillery range in the spring of 1918, and while Congress debated laws meant to override these local considerations, the Thirty-fifth National Guard at Fort Sill, Oklahoma's Camp Doniphan departed for France. Its quarters were used to expand Fort Sill's School of Fire, founded in 1911 as the army's primary field-artillery training and test center. The School of Fire, like the army generally, was unready for entry into the war. In fact, it was closed in 1916 and its personnel sent to augment the tiny peacetime army's strength on the Mexican border. But it had plenty of room and, in nearby Lawton, had civilian hosts so much more unconditionally welcoming than Fremont's that they transferred their federal water right to the army to ensure sufficient water for the men. Lawton did not go dry: the federal government bored new wells, raised the local dam and laid more pipe, allowing residents to

WORLD WAR I ARMY TRAINING BY SAN FRANCISCO BAY

Wouldn't it make you sore?

It took a sense of humor to get through the army. *From* The Twelfth U.S. Infantry—Its Story by Its Men.

do well by doing good in much the way Walter Hoag had done with Camp Fremont's sewers. By October 1917, Fort Sill had fifty thousand acres of maneuver grounds, including a trench field next to its artillery range so that troops could practice placing telephone wires and ordering barrages from the trenches as they would in combat. In June 1918, the army finally acquiesced to French training models and obtained French artillery sufficient for four training centers, including Fort Sill, where entire brigades could be sent. Fremont's Eighth Artillery Brigade was one of three trained at Fort Sill and seven at these centers in all.

The saga of Camp Fremont's artillery reveals many of the challenges America faced in building and fielding an army in seventeen months' time. As Mark Grotelueschen observed, "American divisions ultimately learned how to fight by fighting." Deficiencies in training would be offset by the sheer numbers of men sent abroad. They meant, Faulkner wrote, that "the AEF was not Pershing's master swordsman but rather a blind giant: a creature groping to find its opponent, suffering wound after wound in doing so, but finally crushing the enemy with its superior weight when it finally found him." The delay in training was immaterial in the end to Camp Fremont's

Athletics kept troops busy and built unit cohesion while waiting to deploy. *Menlo Park Historical Association.*

Eighth Division, arriving in France too late to fight. Yet the saga of its artillery is important to understanding the war because it exemplifies the challenge America faced in creating an army almost from scratch and so significantly dependent on public opinion and citizen consent. More than a year after America's war declaration, not only had the nation not begun to train many of its specialized military units, but it was still assembling the land on which to do so.[38]

Extant records do not reveal why the gunners left Camp Fremont after only a few weeks on their hard-won range. The howitzer that exploded in June may not have been locally replaceable. The army may have wearied of blocking traffic, posting warnings to Hotaling's ranch manager or fielding Stanford's complaints over gunners' proximity to its women. Most likely, a spot simply opened up at Fort Sill as the army belatedly moved to centralize its artillery training in line with the growing centralization of the war effort. In any case, by July 11, the army had filled the Eighty-first Field Artillery's vacated quarters off Governor's Avenue with Camp Fremont's developmental battalion, a holding unit primarily for illiterate and non–English speaking soldiers but also for those with disciplinary problems and, occasionally, for venereal patients. It became an ineradicable source of contraband liquor, with officers openly partaking or looking the other way. Records do not reveal whether Stanford liked these new tenants better than the last.

Not everyone with doubts about the war or its local manifestation was as outspoken as Hotaling. Some internalized their dissent or confined it to diaries. Ellen Elliott, the wife of Stanford's registrar, was one of these. When Stanford leased the undeveloped land on the other side of the Elliotts' backyard fence for Camp Fremont, it was declared part of the military reservation and hence off-limits. The army "Keep Out" sign on the Elliotts' back fence became, for the sensitive Ellen, a locus of antiwar meditation. It symbolized the boundary issues and institutional tensions many people around Camp Fremont experienced in having the government enter their lives. The fence reminded Elliott of the great war of her mother's era, the one between the states. Her mother's divided reality was made public and inescapable by having Confederate brothers and a Northern husband. In memoirs published in 1940, Elliott used her mother's distress as metaphor for her own internalized woe: "I don't get reconciled to this war, Mother said soberly. She was a bride when the war of her generation broke out in the 'sixties…It had all come round again, a dreary iteration…And I, too, was a pacifist in principle. Only this once more. War cannot end until Germany is beaten, and this is the war to end war."[39]

Elliott, like many women in the states that then had female suffrage, voted for Wilson in 1916 "because he kept us out of war." Instead, he brought the war to Elliott's backyard. Elliott changed her position on intervention, again in step with many Americans, after Germany announced its resumption of unrestricted submarine warfare on February 1, 1917. Yet her memoir makes clear her ambivalence. She had reason to think her own voice, if raised for peace, would at best be ignored, at worst silenced: "The pacifists in those days were mouse-squeaks, a few people jailed and forgotten, while the dragon's teeth went on being sowed." Female dissenters were not spared prosecution. As the guns boomed beyond Elliott's fence, she could read in her morning *Chronicle* of Rose Pastor Stokes's trial in Missouri for writing that "no government which is *for* the profiteers can also be for the people." Even legal conscientious objectors got short shrift. A Mennonite social worker eventually rescued an Oregon parishioner at Camp Fremont who, instead of receiving noncombatant duty, had been threatened with a bath in human excrement and thrown into the camp jail.[40]

Much nearer to the prevailing spirit was Arthur Kimber, a Stanford junior and close friend of the Elliotts, who left the relative safety of a civilian ambulance unit to become an aviator and was "blown to bits," Elliott wrote, "'in action' over France in September 1918, age twenty-two." Kimber was among the four ambulance drivers from Stanford and the University of California who were tasked in April 1917 with bringing U.S. flags to the Western Front as symbols of support. They received the flags in the great ceremony in San Francisco Civic Auditorium. Kimber and his flag, as it happened, were the first of the four to reach the front in France, notwithstanding an episode in which the flag was briefly kidnapped en route by the Cal drivers. This, plus the bearer's death in action, gave the flag immense sentimental power as the "First Flag" of the rescuing Americans. The French returned Kimber's flag for conveyance to Stanford with the Croix de Guerre pinned to its folds. It stood for decades thus festooned in Stanford Memorial Church, an icon of sentiment in a building itself a monument to youth lost in its prime.[41]

"What could pacifism do in the face of such idealism, such beauty, such young exaltation?" Elliott lamented. "Old women muttered 'I am not reconciled to this war.'" Unable to act on her conscience during the war at hand, she vowed to exhibit more backbone in the next one: "If there is

Stanford junior Arthur Kimber sent a classmate this keepsake of himself with his plane before being shot down over France in September 1918. *Stanford University Archives.*

another [war] before I enter into a peaceful eternity I hope for the privilege of going to jail for refusing to fight it."[42]

A common observation of the U.S. mobilization, then and now, was that it was distant from actual combat. This distance, both geographic and cognitive, allowed Americans to project their values on the situation. Preparedness advocates hailed the value of military training to youth, while many progressives hoped that the wartime government's extended reach would carry social reforms such as improved public health. Young men like Kimber sailed off to war as if it were the Big Game. Depictions of war's pageantry and romance were closer than the war itself and doubtless seemed more real.

Elliott's memoir hints that the war was distant to many Americans in large part because they allowed themselves to think that it was. Living near Camp Fremont disabused some people of that luxury, especially those inclined to nuance and reflection. For Elliott and Hotaling, Camp Fremont brought the war and its ramifications right up to the property line. Their words reveal the homefront's tension in their failure to become reconciled, in Elliott's mother's archaic phrase, to the call that Kimber and so many others answered to bestow their sacrificial gifts.

Just as Camp Fremont encroached on nearby land, it encroached on nearby lives. Female Stanford students resented the strict wartime rules that kept them from walking or riding in cars after dark, lest they be mistaken for the prostitutes who soon were meeting men for assignations in vehicles driven to Camp Fremont's long borders. Such parietal rules were but shadows of the growing regulation of women's conduct around camps and, in part, were

Students called the camp a spur to enlistment. More left for war service than at almost any other coeducational school. *Stanford University Archives.*

aimed to protect Stanford women from this even harsher glare. A subsidiary of the Commission on Training Camp Activities, the War Camp Community Service, in September 1917 created women's boards, billed as "protective," that monitored single women's movements around camps like Fremont. These "protective" boards grew coercive in 1918 after receiving authority to detain and remand women for venereal inspection and treatment. Thirty thousand women nationwide were detained in this way, though only one-third were charged with any crime. A local matron under the auspices of the Committee on Protective Work for Girls prowled San Mateo County for suspicious women, and at least one woman cohabiting with a soldier AWOL from Camp Fremont was tailed by the federal Bureau of Investigation for possible detention.

Still, Camp Fremont's most notable encroachment was on Stanford, which had provided so much of the camp land. Baker and his fellow progressives in Washington envisioned the war cantonments in a larger sense as educating the men and enlarging their sympathies, fitting them for life in a strong and vital America as well as for combat. Asked to provide wholesome and relaxing diversions such as lectures, Stanford worked hard to lift the camp's moral and mental tone. An education professor supervised twenty remedial-

English instructors at Camp Fremont while teaching a full Stanford course load, and the head of Romance Languages led seven colleagues and other instructors as the camp's "director of French." Athletic director Harry Maloney left with an assistant to lead Camp Fremont's sports program. Army delays in acquiring munitions and land on which to use them made team sports vital to building unit cohesion. By war's end, more than two dozen Stanford faculty and staff were working at the camp.

On a more basic level, the camp beckoned male students and staff to enlist, which they did in such numbers that university programs and departments were threatened. One student saw Camp Fremont troops as "recruiting posters come to life." Thanks to articulation agreements between Stanford and the army, fifteen officer candidates and twenty-six privates—roughly 4 percent of Stanford's male enrollment in 1918—went straight from Stanford into the camp in a single month. Stanford's enrollment plunged 28 percent in 1917–18 over the previous year, more than the nationwide wartime decline of 20 percent and much more than almost any other coeducational school. The effect of enlistment, Wilbur observed, was to "practically eliminate the senior class and to deplete the junior and sophomore classes." The University of California, which hosted a much smaller military presence, saw its enrollment drop only 14 percent. By November 1917, Wilbur, who had intoned at June's commencement that "upon America rests much of the burden of replacing in the line those who die in battle," was begging students not to enlist. Marx desperately pulled strings to have science and engineering majors deployed back to campus as reservists so that these departments would have enough students to operate. As the lowering of the draft age loomed, Wilbur and other college presidents lobbied Baker to put "certain students and highly trained men in one of the later draft classifications," only to be told that "such an arrangement would not be in the public interest." As Wilson told MIT's president, "while he [Wilson] might see the benefit of college training, the man on the street could not." Baker had modeled the camps on "the analogy of the American college," and Camp Fremont competed for resources with the campus on which it partly sat. Senator Willard Saulsbury Jr. of Delaware spoke for many as to which entity should win: "There is not much use in educating the young men of this country to be dominated by Huns…It is not so necessary that our colleges shall run for a few months as it is necessary that we should get work done which is necessary for the successful prosecution of the war."[43]

The nation's depleted colleges, including Stanford, were rescued in the war's final weeks. In keeping with the trend, rescue came by government takeover. In September 1918, as Wilson foresaw a shortage of junior officers and technical specialists, 516 schools were paid to militarize their male undergraduates into a federal Student Army Training Corps (SATC) that kept high-potential prospects in a holding pattern until called up. In addition to paying students the enlisted man's $30 monthly, the SATC paid a larger direct subsidy to colleges of $1.48 per man per day. It also reimbursed schools for any expenses related to sequestering SATC men under military discipline. For roughly ten weeks' participation in SATC, Stanford received a new dining hall and a total of $95,790.65, more than it had received for Camp Fremont in a much longer span. Unlike the Camp Fremont rent, university officials noted, this federal money arrived promptly and without fuss.

Even so, the university spent the years after the war in a flurry of redefinition and reform, as if to regain autonomy lost during Camp Fremont's tenure. The financial vulnerability that had helped make the lease tempting was addressed. Soon after the war, trustees imposed tuition and sold the vast Central Valley ranches for investment in commercial loans, creating badly needed income streams. They sought independent clarification of their fiduciary role in relation to the educational mission, a distinction that leasing the camp with all its distractions had muddied. Furthermore, they began after the war, for the first time, to fundraise. Trustee Hoover, who had done so much in war relief and in the Food Administration to plant the idea in Americans' minds that individual giving fueled collective victory, led this innovation. Finally, as if in response to criticism, trustees clarified the distinction between the educational plant and the land today called the "Academic Reserve," which comprised the bulk of the acreage they had made available for the army camp.

Perhaps just as crucial to many people at the time, Stanford's sacrifice of its grounds absolved it of charges of anti-patriotism. "Sniping at the university fell off," Edith Mirrielees recalled. Following the sentiments of the era, much of this redemption derived from the shed blood of Arthur Kimber and Stanford's seventy-six other war dead, the lost soldiers and war workers she dubbed "Stanford's first Honor Roll." Some people in the community praised Stanford's lease of its grounds as a comparable physical sacrifice, a pledge of the corporate body. One writer saw in the foothills' withstanding of artillery bombardments a metaphor for America's resilience and was comforted for the war's toll by the endurance of Stanford's stately oak trees. The problem of managing land that had been used as munitions grounds lay decades in the future.[44]

As artillery bombardments of his cattle pastures commenced in the spring of 1918, Hotaling wrote his own ambivalence into a Bohemian Club masque on the global conflict:

> *Hereafter, should the cry for battle fill the air,*
> *it shall be left for those whose blood*
> *shall be spilled to vote war's declaration.*
> *Let those who rule hereafter* [be] *selected by the people,*
> *and even then let them be hedged about*
> *by super-councils of the wise and true…*
> *a Parliament of All the Lands*
> *where bloodless wars are waged.*[45]

Club members performed the masque with its many accompanying toasts at their Bohemian Grove in Sonoma County on August 3, 1918. Camp Fremont's Eighth Division trained for its divisional maneuvers the following weekend on Stanford land, while that very day, its commanding general, William S. Graves, received the telegram that would send him to Siberia.

Chapter 3

WAR AS OPPORTUNITY

Locals Find Roles in the Great Adventure

Despite the ambivalence of people like Richard Hotaling and Ellen Elliott, most Peninsula residents seem to have been happy Camp Fremont was there. They found a way to make it serve their aims. If nothing else, the camp offered novelty and a market for local goods and services. Locals strove to prove their patriotism by making the troops welcome and giving them what they wanted, though conflict ensued when what the troops wanted most was alcohol and sex.

Many people in and around Camp Fremont craved something else, just as seductive. They craved opportunity. They sought roles that the war and the camp created in military technology, healthcare, social services and management. These locals reveal how war carries social and technological change via soldiers and civilians alike, as well as the anxiety such change often brings. Their stories resonate today because hindsight is 20/20, and we can see these tank drivers, aid administrators and healthcare providers as the vanguard of the industrial and service economy of twentieth-century America. They also resonate because these pioneers, mostly young, were brave.

Army nurse Muriel Hamilton tasted adventure but also risk in caring for the highly contagious patients who packed Camp Fremont's hospital after the influenza epidemic reached the Bay Area on September 24, 1918. She wrote her family: "So far as the danger is concerned it gives you the creeps to think that you might never come home, and also that you might come less than a wreck, but one can't think long of those things and after all, what is life, anyhow! There is an awful lot of 'living' that I don't call life."

Hamilton lived under military discipline but was no slave to authority. She ducked her supervisors when possible, especially Miss Gill, the redoubtable chief nurse, who "laid out flat" a hapless nurse who flirted with one of the French training officers assigned to the camp. Hamilton regarded the flimsy, wood-frame camp hospital as the "last minute" in healthcare, in the slang of the era, and herself as helping smash a status quo of medical ignorance, "slack" hygiene and "doubtful cleanliness." At Camp Fremont, she lived first in a tent and then in a barn left behind by Walter Hoag's previous tenants. Nurses in army service were treated as if of officer rank, and enlisted men were not supposed to fraternize with them. Hamilton took such rules lightly. The nurse shortage meant she could. Her catchphrase in letters home to Ontario, California, was "I should worry."

> *One of the Base 50 boys has gotten out a mirror and is flashing it in the sun at me and pretty much blinding me, and I hope he'll get tired of it pretty soon. There is also a report that a buck private got 30 days in the guardhouse for taking a nurse to a movie and that the officers have been detailed to watch me hereafter! Isn't that the limit! I should worry!...Every other night or so we go down to the Y and sing to our hearts' content with the boys we are not allowed to be seen talking to.*

She was twenty-four and having the time of her life. "They're having a class in French tonight but I'm too lazy to go clear down all those boardwalks past all those eyes...We should worry. As I said, soldiers work for us and wait on the table and swab out our dorm. They don't care whether we are in bed or dressing or anything, so we don't either—it wouldn't do any good if we did."

On days off, Hamilton rode horseback across downtown Palo Alto in pants, an item of dress that Stanford forbade women to wear to class or on the Quad for another fifty years:

> *I've been cogitating all thro this letter whether to tell you what I did Sunday PM and have decided to risk it. It was such fun. I* rode *in my* breeches *on a beautiful white horse right down the middle of Palo Alto with millions of automobiles—trains and soldiers and everything. I was perfectly unafraid and managed beautiful but can't get over where I got my nerve.*

Security in her skills gave her confidence. Hamilton was a "special," or in today's terms, a critical-care nurse. In an era when doctors had few remedies against infectious disease, skilled nursing care was many patients' best chance for survival. Charged with as few as three patients at a time, Hamilton rolled them in icy sheets to reduce their fevers, kept them hydrated and injected them with doubtful drugs that were considered state-of-the-art. Yet even Hamilton's high spirits were tested by the epidemic:

> *Dearest family, I wrote a melancholy letter one night a few days ago but in the morning decided not to send it. One of our prettiest jolliest nurses was dying that night—she died the next morning—and seven men died in my ward that day. There are about 35* [nurses] *altogether sick—most of them I know well. I lend nightgowns to sick nurses...and uniforms to tired well nurses who otherwise would have to rinse out and iron their own.*

She did not stay melancholy for long. For Hamilton and many young people like her, the war brought freedom and new experiences that mitigated any suffering. "I'm not going back to private nursing in a hurry. It would be fun to go to Egypt or Italy or Siberia or Germany or France or Camp Lewis or an Eastern Camp or somewhere...One thing, I've made more friends here than I ever did anywhere before."[46]

As Hamilton rode in her scandalous pants through downtown Palo Alto, she was conscious of moving among people who seemed much less energized by change. In fact, some of these people would view the war as an opportunity to uphold the status quo, not smash it. Ruth Taylor became a lightning rod for such tensions as the first female editor of Stanford's daily newspaper. Vivacious and adventurous, unafraid of being ahead of her time, Taylor exemplified many American women who filled jobs men had left for war.

For decades, most female journalists worked on "women's sections" that went to press early in the evening and were compatible with curfews and notions of propriety. Taylor, however, rose through the *Daily*'s main ranks just behind her brother Frank, who left in 1918 to become a war correspondent with the AEF. When enlistments thinned Stanford's male enrollment, Ruth Taylor's peers voted her to the top spot. Taylor's Tri Delt sisters decorated the chapter-house parlor to resemble what a newsroom would look like if news were the purview of women: spittoons filled with roses instead of tobacco juice, typewriters nestled on doilies. Soon, though, Taylor crossed swords with Stanford's dean of women, Harriet Bradford. Editing late news meant violating

Nurse Lyons of Camp Fremont's hospital enjoys a quiet moment. *Menlo Park Historical Association, Hazel Rasor scrapbook.*

parietal rules tightened by Camp Fremont's presence, notably the "motor rule," which banned female students from riding or driving in cars after dark. As editor-in-chief, Taylor trained and mentored men and passed editorial judgment on the male-dominated events that streamed from the news wires. "The Dean of Women claimed it was no job for a lady," Taylor wrote in a family memoir. She left Stanford for good in her senior year.

Ruth Taylor became the Stanford *Daily*'s first female editor when qualified men left for war service. The cap may be from her brother Frank, a war correspondent in France. *Taylor family collection.*

To the infuriated staff of the *Daily*, Bradford and similarly thinking people formed a bulwark of reaction—dangerous, backward and inimical to the war effort. Their faculty adviser cast the issue as one of selfishness stemming progressivism's mighty tide. "Undergraduate newspaper men have gone away to war heroically against an insidious enemy. The women come forward and labor with intense zeal…Personal prejudices appear to have risen above the common welfare. Is such an attitude… the heralded Stanford spirit? Did…Camp Fremont claim it all?"[47]

Taylor rebounded from Bradford's scorn, becoming a successful news artist and illustrator. Ironically, considering the difficulty that wartime curbs on women's mobility caused her, she came to specialize in making maps. As automobile tourism soared in the 1920s and 1930s, she became known for cartoon-studded maps of Hawaii and other tourist destinations. Highly collectable today, her best-known work is called *A Gay Geography*.

Still, concerns like Bradford's about vice and propriety were not unfounded. Hosting an army division of twenty-eight thousand soldiers raised legitimate concerns. Unsavory tales abounded of carousing troops on the Mexican border, where several Camp Fremont units had recently served. The army left it largely to camp localities to keep troops more wholesomely occupied and to provide them with social services. The YMCA and War Camp Community Service, staffed locally by volunteers, were among many groups charged with these tasks. War Secretary Baker urged Americans to gird camp communities in an "invisible armor." He called for "a realization of the community responsibility for the lives of people who live in it and near it…by what it has done for the stranger within its gates, than it has ever had before." The thickness of this armor varied by community, and so did the services offered. One pious Midwest town expelled a War Camp Community Service worker who proposed that movies be shown on the Sabbath.[48]

In Palo Alto, one resource was the local chapter of the National Defenders Club, a nationwide network of civilians in areas with military installations. The Palo Alto Defenders Club offered troops a quiet, alcohol-free lounge off University Avenue. The Defenders, who were mostly middle- to upper-middle-class clubwomen, also raised money for Camp Fremont recreation, the army having ceded this function as well to local volunteers. For such women, Nancy Bristow argues, the opportunity posed by the war was one of cementing class distinctions and upholding the status quo. They were high-handed, even competitive, in their efforts to pry money from neighbors for wartime initiatives ranging from Liberty Bonds to cigarettes and tennis rackets for the troops. They outraged Dean Bradford by suggesting that Stanford sororities "keep open house" for "men whom they do not know, except [that] they are the American army." Not coincidentally, the Defenders Club was an excellent place to find an officer husband. The 319th Engineers' top officers, Major James A. Dorst and Colonel Curtis W. Otwell, both married women who had raised money for instruments for the regimental band through the Palo Alto Defenders Club.[49]

Morals in that time were thought to correlate with class. Nationwide, civic leaders feared camps would attract "charity girls," working-class women "hysterical at the sight of buttons and uniforms," as the Commission on Training Camp Activities' Raymond Fosdick put it, who might sleep with soldiers in exchange for an evening's fun. Camp Fremont was "a bonanza," remembered Louise Mann, then a child in Palo Alto: "Boys, and more boys." This was not the kind of opportunity that civic leaders hoped to foster. The Palo Alto City Council voted in July 1917 to require a separate permit for each dance held in the city, thereby raising ticket prices beyond what a shopgirl or waitress could pay. Across the creek in San Mateo County, however, many greeted the wartime vice crackdown with chagrin. "Liquor dealers are very much worried" by the Selective Service Act's five-mile dry zone, the *Redwood City Democrat* reported. Unlike in Palo Alto across the county line, dance promoters in San Mateo County could operate merely by personal consent of any one of the county Board of Supervisors. One promoter evaded even this low bar by structuring his nightly entertainments as a business called the "Fremont Dancing Academy."[50]

National security around camps, like the provision of social services, also relied on the energy of civic volunteers. Tasked by the wartime government to root out vice and sabotage, citizens near Camp Fremont and elsewhere often used authority granted under watchdog groups like the American Protective League to pursue their own goals. The league's 250,000 members became amateur spies for the federal Bureau of Investigation, precursor to today's FBI. Looking at the more than 130 reports that Bay Area members generated for federal authorities, one often sees their health and security concerns masking private agendas and being used to settle old scores. Such civilians cited progressivism in their desire to clean up their neighborhoods. The progressive intellectual Walter Weyl, disillusioned at the turn that the movement had taken, dubbed such activities "the illusion of progress" in his 1921 recap of the war.[51]

A Palo Alto lumber retailer peppered his Protective League contact in San Jose with complaints of illegal alcohol sales, including the thriving trade at Camp Fremont's developmental battalion headquarters. He was appalled when a captain replied "that he did not want to pursue this angle of the investigation, because it would be far-reaching." Anyone could file a report on a neighbor with

Hostess House, designed by noted architect Julia Morgan, allowed troops to meet sweethearts or female relatives in comfort. *Menlo Park Historical Association, Hazel Rasor scrapbook.*

Moved to Palo Alto after the war, Hostess House became America's first municipal community center and later the MacArthur Park restaurant. *Stanford University Archives.*

the nearest post office. One Palo Altan swore out an affidavit against her former employer, a grocer at Emerson Street and University Avenue who had had the bad luck to be born in Austria. Events pointed "strongly to the probability that he has been selling liquor to soldiers," the affiant claimed. She recommended that the government put a tail on his delivery wagon. "Further she states that the delivery boy who drives this wagon is crooked. He is part German and part Spanish and goes by the name of Toots."[52]

Many such reports seem to have been filed and forgotten, but Palo Alto's postmaster forwarded to investigators a shopkeeper's report on a Waverly Street woman whose work giving classes "in German or French" made her an object of suspicion. "Complainant says Mrs. Diesel called up to give him an order, then told him over the phone that 'the Kaiser is not near so bad as President Wilson, and one government is as good as another.'" Camp Fremont's intelligence office placed both Mrs. Diesel and her husband under investigation for "disloyal utterances" in violation of the Espionage Act.[53]

Many thoughtful people, including Stanford's Ellen Elliott, tried to analyze the tension of the times and found it partly generational. Elliott's own distaste for war was influenced by her parents' experience in the Civil War. She understood why young people lacking this perspective had fewer reservations and ventured out to save a world gone mad. In contrast, many members of "the skipped generation," as the Committee on Public Information dubbed the middle-aged in a Red Cross recruitment ad, underwent a complex mixture of feelings as they saw young men off to battle. Some envied the spotlight's shift to the young.

The CPI had a cure for this midlife malaise. "Men of large affairs" who answered the call for Red Cross service, the CPI argued, need not feel passed over. Applying their managerial talents overseas, they could rescue "starving little children" and "mothers numb with horror" in a "great net of mercy drawn through an ocean of unspeakable pain." It was a new and heroic role and an implicitly political one, because it depended on and projected America's new geopolitical force. Herbert Hoover was the template for this type of civilian, and thousands followed his cue. Among them was cattleman D.O. Lively, formerly the Panama-Pacific International Exposition's director of livestock. Lively was cast at loose ends when the army took over his acreage for Camp Fremont's artillery range. He became an international aid executive at the age of fifty, coupling his skills with adventure that life behind a desk had denied him.

As New Year's Day 1920 dawned on the Siberian port city of Vladivostok, Lively, division manager of the American National Red Cross, penned a cheery list of New Year's resolutions for his staff. Harried by U.S. civilians seeking repatriation, if not by the Bolsheviks who would in four weeks impose martial law, Lively urged his team to resolve that "sunshine and cheerfulness shall be your playmates." Czechs aligned with anti-Bolshevik Russians, the very people Woodrow Wilson sent five thousand Camp Fremont men to protect, were extorting large sums from Lively's staff in one part of the interior. A blockade in the name of the Allies hindered aid distributions elsewhere. Wilson's Russian *aide-memoire* allowed U.S. troops not only to guard Czech forces but also to "steady any efforts at self-government or self-defense in which the Russians themselves may be willing to accept assistance." Lively's mission thus gave aid and moral camouflage to military action against people with whom America was not at war and whom Lively found friendly and grateful for help. Yet such chaos and ambiguity, Lively chided, was no reason for his workers to be cross. "I represent the antithesis of intolerance," he urged them to pledge in the coming year. "Individual ingratitude or local indifference," he wrote, "shall not deter me from carrying forward the spirit of the Greatest Mother in the world."[54]

Lively's first post upon leaving San Francisco in the autumn of 1918 was the Arctic port of Archangel, where the Red Cross ran a hospital for the

4,500 troops in Wilson's North Russian intervention. It also furnished daily hot lunches for 23,000 Russian children. For this work, Lively was awarded the Order of St. Stanislaus with crossed swords by the local White Russian government. Other benefits materialized as Lively drew up his great net of Red Cross mercy. "Cruising in a trawler through the ice-filled White Sea," according to the *New York Times*, "he carried food to starving refugees on the Kola Peninsula. One of the refugees was Erna Lazda, who had escaped from Riga. They were married in June, 1921."[55]

From Archangel, Lively and Erna went with the Red Cross to Vladivostok, where Lively oversaw the running of medical trains as far into the Siberian interior as Russia's unstable political situation would allow. Lively disbursed some $3 million in supplies. He remained with a skeleton crew after most civilians and the last of the U.S. troops, including the Camp Fremont men, embarked for San Francisco in April 1920 after White Russian leader Alexander Kolchak's capitulation. It was dangerous: the chief engineer of a U.S. aid transport was shot in the back on Orthodox Christmas Day 1921 after leaving a holiday celebration.

Lively remained in Siberia because he had found a mission within a mission. He had tasked himself with returning nine hundred children from Russian famine zones who had been entrusted to the Red Cross by relatives and brought to Vladivostok, where there was food. "When you consider that the trip is over 6,000 miles and through a country that is short on food and rife with typhus," he wrote a colleague, "you will see that we have a lot of things to think about and preparations to make." The adventure was addictive, and Lively never returned to the for-profit sector. He became Far East commissioner of the U.S. Department of Agriculture and then served as national director of China Famine Relief from 1928 until his death in 1933.[56]

One could argue that on one level not much in Lively's life had changed. He was still cutting deals and dispatching freight cars, although they now carried displaced children and medical supplies instead of cattle. What had changed were the parameters of success. Instead of accumulating capital, he was saving lives; instead of making money, he was asking for it. It was "a new vision in the administration of business," Lively marveled, one that offered "no permanence in the job, no visible returns from the money spent and often no means of definitely telling whether or not the supplies were intelligently used." Presence, rather than verifiable result, was paramount in this expression of America's new overseas power. Direct beneficiaries such as orphans were remote and largely voiceless, but the way in which their aid was perceived and leveraged had global ramifications.[57]

Still, the chief hero of the day was the humble combat soldier. Camp Fremont's delay in deployment meant the camp lacked many of these. Yet the camp's arguably most renowned soldier was a true combat hero, the kind of man many Americans hoped to become in 1918. Although Corporal Harold W. Roberts was not in camp for long, the story of this native San Franciscan came to inspire people throughout the nation. It deserves to be retold.

Roberts transferred into the new Tank Corps in early 1918 as his campmates drilled and dug trenches while waiting to deploy. He died in October at the controls of this new military weapon. Ambushed in a flooded shell crater

Heavy motorized transport was in its infancy, mechanically and logistically, when the Tank Corps formed in 1918. *National Archives.*

during the Meuse-Argonne offensive, he pushed his gunner out the tank's only functioning door and told him, "There's only room for one of us to get out—and out you go!" Roberts posthumously received the Medal of Honor and became famous in the postwar years for his melodramatic death at the helm of a new machine. Camp Roberts in central California is named for him.

He was born William Harold Roberts in the city's Noe Valley neighborhood. His mother's parents were German, and his biographer surmises that he swapped his first and middle names to forestall teasing over sharing a name with the Kaiser. Many German Americans went to great lengths to prove their patriotism, which was unsurprising at a time when teachers and grocers were pitilessly followed for signs of espionage. Of nearly two hundred army inductees from one San Francisco draft office who were high school graduates and whose records are preserved in the National Archives, 80 percent reported speaking German at home.

In 1916, as tanks debuted on the Western Front and as San Francisco roiled over military preparedness, Roberts left the University of California to join the army. He ended up in the Fifteenth Cavalry and, whatever he may have intended, was sent to the Philippines, where America maintained a presence after the Spanish-American War. The Fifteenth was one of three cavalry units moved in late 1917 and early 1918 to Camp Fremont, where Roberts's unit awaited further developments and the others became machine gun units. Items on the Tank Corps ran that winter in the *Palo Alto Daily Times* and other local papers. Writers labored to convey the tanks' lumbering strangeness and their power to knock down trees and traverse battle trenches. "The Samson of machinery," one writer called them, "toads of a vast size emerging from the primeval slime in the twilight of the world's dawn." For a bored soldier stuck in the pastures of Camp Fremont, they offered a chance to try something new. Ironically, Roberts's Fifteenth Cavalry was mobilized just a few weeks after his transfer, becoming one of very few Camp Fremont units to see action.[58]

Sent to France in the summer of 1918, Roberts was assigned to Company A of the 344th Light Tank Battalion, 1st Division, 304th Tank Brigade, and promoted to corporal in the fall. The tanks were the French FT-17 Renaults that had so surprised German machine gun nests in July at the second Battle of the Marne and prompted mass surrenders. Tiny but innovative, they were operated by a driver and a gunner who practically sat on the driver's shoulders. They were French-built; while the United States had contracted to build 1,200 Renaults and 4,800 tanks in all, only 15 reached France before the Armistice. Their production was stalled by the same disorganization that hindered U.S.

warplane manufacture and Camp Fremont's artillery program. The French themselves struggled to maintain the tanks at a time when motorized heavy transport was in its infancy. Up to half of France's tanks were out of service at any time for lack of parts.

Corporal Harold W. Roberts left Camp Fremont for the Tank Corps and a heroic end in the Meuse-Argonne. *San Francisco History Center, San Francisco Public Library.*

Roberts's tank arrived two weeks before his battalion's initial action. The men were told to strap two fifty-five-gallon drums of gasoline to the rear of each vehicle to help with the logistics of fueling. Should the tank be hit, the men were told, the strap would disintegrate under fire and cause the drums to roll safely away. U.S. Tank Corps commander Colonel George S. Patton fielded more than one hundred Renaults in the AEF's Saint-Mihiel offensive in September and then sent them along with 600,000 exhausted soldiers to the much larger Meuse-Argonne operation that began eleven days later. By that time, the Germans had learned to exploit the Renault's weaknesses by repurposing shell craters as ambushes.

Sergeant Virgil Morgan, Roberts's gunner, tells what happened next. On October 4, 1918, their company advanced under heavy fire in the Meuse-Argonne's Montrebeau Woods. Ahead lay a mass of foliage that seemed, in the dim vision that the tank allowed, to hide enemy machine guns. They drove in only to find themselves in a trap, upside down and sinking:

> *By keeping the engine running in the reverse was our only way to keep the rear of the tank above the water. As it took the continuous care of one man to keep the thing going, only one of us could get out. Roberts was in charge of the tank...I did the best I could to make him go himself, and wanted to*

> *stay with him when we were in so much trouble, but when I insisted that I stay, he said: "Go, get out of here," and I went.*[59]

With water flooding the vehicle, Roberts said his heroic last words and pushed Morgan away. Morgan was unable to rescue him under the heavy fire but returned as soon as possible to find Roberts had drowned.

In death, Roberts became headline news. He was featured on postcards and in children's books, always with his tank. A newspaper ad for the Victory Liberty Loan portrayed him in his final struggle as a hand reaching vainly from the engulfing muck, the tank much larger than in reality. "Corporal Roberts gave his life coolly, deliberately for you," the ad read. "Make good his sacrifice. Invest to the very limit of your cash and resources." Tanks were shipped around the country as promotional props for the Victory Loan, the war's final fundraising campaign. Morgan finished his service by posing with them and telling Roberts's story.[60]

Corporal Harold W. Roberts was one of some fifty-three thousand Americans killed in action in World War I, half of them in the Meuse-Argonne. He was one of at least nine Medal of Honor recipients in the Meuse-Argonne, still after a century America's largest battle and its costliest in military lives. His valor is timeless, but his story resonated in 1918 among many great deeds for what it said about the times. It hinted that the industrial war Americans had just won was not an episode to be put behind them, but a taste of a grim future in which machines like Roberts's tank might defy human control. "In the superwar, which the next war must inescapably be, the skies will be thick with battle," *Collier's* predicted. "Armadas of super-Gothas and Aviatiks will slay their tens of thousands… where their feeble predecessors now kill women by the score." In this future, change was not always good, and not everyone was prepared to face it as bravely as Corporal Roberts or D.O. Lively or Muriel Hamilton had done. Harold Roberts's story revealed that even victory brought risks and fears that defied easy containment. Such risks and fears could not be corralled into submission in the way that the American Protective League and other citizens had tried to monitor behavior around camps like Fremont. Some locals used war aims to project their anxieties about immigrants, women's growing freedom and other social forces. Others, like Roberts, seized the day and forged memorable advances.[61]

Chapter 4

"HE WILL COME BACK A BETTER MAN!"

Health and the 1918 Influenza Epidemic

Camp Fremont's hospital lay two miles from the main camp, near the main road, Willow Road, that links Menlo Park and San Francisco Bay. Immediately south of the hospital across Willow Road was the camp remount station, where the more than five thousand horses and mules that did the camp's hauling were kept. This proximity was unusual but not unique among World War I training camps; Camp Bowie, near Fort Worth, was laid out in almost exactly the same way. Through the hospital grounds ran the $55,000 sewer outfall to the bay that had been financed by San Francisco's citizens committee. Neither the remount station nor even the entire hospital, like the bulk of the main camp itself, had its toilets connected to this sewer line during the war. Instead, the people in these places used latrines, and the manure from the remount station was hauled by a contractor to the bay and dumped there. Every month, the camp's sanitary inspectors issued a detailed report ending with a complaint that the army had not connected camp privies to the sewer line. Every month, this complaint was ignored, the government having determined early in the war that National Guard camps such as Camp Fremont were meant to be temporary and that long-term sanitation improvements were therefore unnecessary. The hospital kitchens and washrooms were hooked up to the sewer, but there were no washing machines to do the laundry, and so it was sent out to private contractors.

The hospital itself was an unadorned and deceptively modern-looking collection of well-ventilated wooden buildings, "all paper-roofed, rustic and low, like so many bricks," as one patient recalled them. They were linked by covered boardwalks against frequent seepage in the low-lying soil that fronted the bay. Rosalie Stern, associate field director of the local Red Cross, brought in landscape architect Ralph McLaren, who had designed Golden Gate Park, to provide restful and fragrant plantings. Stern's concern for the camp and its hospital were constant and thorough. She opened her summer home—one of the first on the Peninsula to have a swimming pool—to informal afternoons for the soldiers, made a floor of her San Francisco home into a Red Cross office with stations for sewing pajamas and, when the influenza pandemic reached Camp Fremont in late September 1918, personally guaranteed on behalf of the Red Cross the salary difference between army and civilian nurses to help ease the nurse shortage in the crowded army wards. Coal stoves and wood fires heated the hospital, a fact briefly implicated in the other—luckily not fatal—crisis to hit Camp Fremont, at 3:30 a.m. on September 13, 1918. For in all the camp, with its thousands of wood fires and the thousands of cigarette-smoking soldiers who sat around them, it was a section of the hospital that burned during the first fall rains. The fire, later deduced to be electrical in origin, was confined to one building. The more than one thousand people on the grounds were evacuated or accounted for quickly and safely, a remarkable accomplishment. Much altered, the hospital remains in use today as the Department of Veterans Affairs' Menlo Park campus. Two buildings survive from the Camp Fremont era, generic structures used during the war as a chapel and a morgue.[62]

Camp Fremont's hospital, and the camp's health and safety measures generally, allow us to compare the era's progressive medical and public-health goals with progress toward those goals—between the government's presentation of army life as a font of social benefits and how soldiers really lived. Surgeon General William C. Gorgas entered the war hoping to "make a record for our country in the sanitation of our new armies." The Committee on Public Information reassured soldiers' families that "He Will Come Back a Better Man!" with "newer and better equipment, in mind and body—fitting him for a bigger, finer life." Healthcare was one arena in which the ideology of progressivism that fueled so much of the U.S. war effort eventually produced measurable results. The war yielded national health statistics that provided both a baseline and an impetus for future efforts. Army authorities claimed a reduction in venereal disease through prevention and treatment. They treated diseases such as tuberculosis when they were found in inductees, and they provided mass inoculations against smallpox and typhoid. Inductees' anxious reactions to the shots and exams indicate that they were being exposed to a level of healthcare that they had not experienced before. Their discomfort can be seen as growing pains of the nation's improving health.[63]

The fire and the flu at Camp Fremont also reveal how soldiers and the institutions that led them reacted to danger. Very few Camp Fremont troops saw action in the war, most being mobilized just weeks before the Armistice. For many, the epidemic and, to a much lesser extent, the fire were the most dramatic things that happened to them in the army. As people often did wherever on Earth the epidemic struck, the soldiers tended to conflate the flu with the war, and the epidemic figured strongly in their wartime reminiscences. The War Department took risks with its troops, including Camp Fremont's, by mobilizing them at the height of the epidemic in hope of ending the war quickly by pouring in the maximum strength of men. It took similar risks by not providing adequate fire protection in camp, again citing the need to weight its resources in favor of the men on the front. Some men were able to assimilate their assumption of these risks into a

The wooden pavilions of Camp Fremont's hospital made few concessions to fire safety because they were meant to be occupied a short time. *Menlo Park Historical Association.*

narrative of wartime bravado and sacrifice. Others just felt sick, miserable and wronged, and their accounts provide a counter-narrative to the army's "credit side of the war ledger," as Gorgas put it: the assertion that the rising robustness and power of America as a nation stood in symbiosis to the rising robustness and power of its individual men.

Moreover, Camp Fremont's health and safety workers kept such good records that they provide information difficult to find elsewhere. We know, for example, that although the camp's principal contractor told the army that it entrained construction workers daily from San Francisco to the camp, many workers lived in squatter camps along San Francisquito Creek and on the hospital grounds. Although the camp had largely been built by mid-1918, there was still ongoing construction and maintenance to be done, and many other services, such as waste hauling and hospital laundry, were performed not by the army but by civilians under contract. Some of these civilians supplemented their incomes with side jobs, such as peddling fruit to the soldiers. Along with the flies from the remount station, the civilian squatters gave the monthly health and fire inspectors a constant headache, with their food-waste litter, their shacks and outhouses and their cooking fires. One inspector recommended clearing up one such "hoboes' retreat" and dispersing the occupants. Camp Fremont's fire marshal, Captain William Potter, in some ways more tolerant, replied:

> *Outhouse is used by carpenters of Lindgren and Co...Some poor laborers have built the shack mentioned...and are occupying it from necessity, not choice...so far as I can see,* [it] *is not a menace. It is hidden in the brush in order that shade may be enjoyed. The tin cans scattered around are dry, and are not unclean so far as I can see. I would hesitate before tearing down this shack and removing the cans under the circumstances.*

Captain Potter, whose quarters were among the few at Camp Fremont that were blessed with modern plumbing, added, "I might add that we do not allow civilians to use our toilets." The squatters also turn up in the investigation of the hospital fire, which was finally deduced to be a short-circuit of exposed wiring resulting from heavy rain.[64]

The camp's carefully kept statistics reveal the ubiquity of infectious disease in early twentieth-century America. About half the camp's hospital patients were admitted with measles, mumps, tuberculosis or the pneumonia that often developed from these diseases. All were dangerous in the days before antibiotics or the relevant vaccines. Four to seventeen men died at the camp each month before the epidemic. More than half were infectious-disease cases. Such diseases came in waves and prompted a succession of quarantine measures, such as the closing of motion-picture theaters after a measles outbreak in August 1918. The men remembered the quarantines as increasing in severity and therefore in annoyance. Also represented were appendicitis, car-crash injuries and, occasionally, wounds from knife fights. Training accidents such as bayonet wounds accounted for one or two beds a month.

The rest of Camp Fremont's sick roll was of a motley range that seemed to take up an inordinate share of the army's medical and ideological attention and thus of the medical records. It included men with stomach pains, common colds and transient symptoms that could be interpreted as malingering and thus required suspicious watching. It also included the venereal cases. Venereal disease was a paramount concern of the War Department and one it had spent considerable resources trying to fight, including founding the Commission on Training Camp Activities just days after the war declaration, with its comprehensive program of what historian Nancy Bristow called "recreation, prevention and repression." Only 4 percent of the army's VD cases were incurred while in service, the surgeon general was proud to report after the war. The rest—259,612 men or roughly 5 percent of America's eventual wartime troop strength—had had the disease upon induction and were held in casual camps, developmental battalions or some other holding pattern pending completion of an unpleasant treatment that took several weeks. A soldier who caught VD while in service had defied a long gauntlet of warnings. He, like the malingerer, was a threat to the army's mission because he was presumed to be a moral shirker who compromised the army's will to fight. He required a good deal of the army's attention, not only for treatment and potential discipline—since failing to report for prophylaxis after potential exposure was a court-martial offense—but also for a good deal of public shame.[65]

The new VD patient was "carded" with a long list of prohibited activities, and his pay was stopped for the duration of treatment. At Camp Fremont, he was specifically banned from wards with female nurses, less to protect the nurses than to increase his shame. In a pamphlet mass-produced for troops, a corporal with syphilis reads his "VD card" and broods to an army physician on his curtailed life prospects:

> *"'Don't kiss anybody. Don't let another use your pipe, spoon, fork, drinking cup. Don't touch your eyes after you have handled the sex organs. Don't marry till you know you're cured…'*

Some commanding officers thought the hospital was for slackers seeking narcotics and the company of female nurses. Note the patient smoking (far right). *Menlo Park Historical Association.*

> *"You think, then, Major, that I will be all right, say, in six or eight years?"*
> *"Think? I am 99/100ths sure of it, and it ought not to take any such time, either, if you stick at it."*[66]

If failing to report for treatment could be a disciplinary offense, so, too, was seeking treatment in excess of what the army was inclined to give. Some on Camp Fremont's hospital staff felt their unit was a magnet for malingerers seeking narcotics and the company of female nurses. One infantryman recalled that "CC pills"—calomel and codeine, the former a mercury compound given as a laxative and disinfectant—"were an all-purpose nostrum for everything from rheumatism to toothache." A Camp Fremont private complained to his CO about being scolded for his perceived taste for narcotics: "I was told in a loud voice that all I was looking for was a 'shot' of morphine and the captain on duty implying that I was a habitual user of that drug." Despite the scornful staff's diagnosis of "autointoxication," he received a CC pill just the same, plus one for the road.[67]

Hospitalized soldiers were considered separated from their units, so there could be a certain reluctance to let them go. If the unit were to be deployed—a fond hope at Camp Fremont in the long, dusty days of summer 1918—the hospitalized men would have to be left behind. Even so, Camp Fremont's commanders almost immediately usurped for office space the buildings that had been designed into each regiment's square footage for regimental infirmaries. By the summer of 1918, the health inspectors claimed, the lack of such treatment facilities was putting undue stress on the hospital. The hospitals had been designed to hold 3 percent of a camp's population, but that figure more than doubled at Camp Fremont even before the epidemic. Sickbeds soon filled the hallways and the screened porches that looked out onto Menlo Park's majestically spreading oak trees.

In two-week "Casual Camps" before their assignment to companies, inductees received immunizations and antiseptic throat sprays, were screened for VD and were given time to develop immunity to one another's diseases. Preventive care was key to Gorgas's "credit side of the war ledger." To many inductees, it was clearly a novelty. The three shots against smallpox and typhoid given in Casual Camp occasioned nearly the only complaints of physical discomfort that men ever made in accounts of Camp Fremont life, besides the suffocating two-mile march in gas masks up Sand Hill Road to the trench maneuver ground. "Being shot…in the arm three times," as one soldier put it, generated considerable anxiety among a population in which vaccination was not yet routine.[68]

Men who did end up in hospital tended to stay a long time, since recovery from many conditions took weeks in an era when bed rest was the chief available treatment. The ever-vigilant Commission on Training Camp Activities feared that long-term patients could get bored. A large, wooden open-air theater was built near Camp Fremont's hospital receiving ward, again deceptively modern to twenty-first-century eyes, with its roof supported by banks of wooden scaffolding resembling the sound towers of modern pop concerts. Photos show soldiers attending events there eclectically dressed in donated Red Cross pajamas and brimmed khaki hats. The hospital was rarely as heavily guarded as its commanders would have preferred and, despite its theater and other diversions, sustained "considerable traffic of liquor" and of "immoral women," as well as theft. Quarters were built for forty-eight nurses and twenty-four medical personnel of officer rank, but these, too, were almost immediately inadequate, and additional officers and nurses slept, like Muriel Hamilton, in dozens of tents pitched on the hospital grounds.[69]

Local philanthropists built a Garden Theater, also of wood, to keep patients entertained during long convalescences. *Menlo Park Historical Association, Hazel Rasor scrapbook.*

The army nurses were an adventuresome sort, however, and Hamilton was not the only one to remember Camp Fremont with enjoyment. They photographed one another wading in the bay marshes east of the hospital in their hours off, watching the waterfowl burst from the rushes at their approach. One nurse, M.J. Roche, later transferred to a mobile hospital attached to the First British Army and received the Ribbon of Merit from the British government for "services performed in the face of grave danger" in the Meuse-Argonne. Wrote the *New York Times*: "Miss Roche was administering an anesthetic in an amputation case when a shell burst outside the operating room. She kept right on with her work." A Camp Fremont lab technician, trying to imagine conditions at the front, asked her soldier brother how nurses in the AEF wore their hair. He replied, "Several of them have swell pompadours, while others do as the soldiers do," coping with the ubiquitous lice and filth by cropping their hair to the army regulation three-quarters of an inch and wearing rubber boots and trousers like the men.[70]

It could be argued that the patients in Camp Fremont's hospital were lucky to receive care under a roof at all, let alone in a heated room. All the National Guard cantonment hospitals were originally planned as tent hospitals, just as the men in most of these camps lived under canvas. These hospital tents, "along with the department hospitals, field hospitals, etc.,

Army nurses celebrated the independence of living away from home and meeting interesting people. *Menlo Park Historical Association, Hazel Rasor scrapbook.*

[and other] equipment...had been slowly acquired after years of planning and effort," according to the surgeon general's official medical history, and thus reflected the medical practice of previous years and wars. As parceled out to the camps in the early months of U.S. intervention, this equipment was inadequate from the start. When "the question of adequate hospital provision had been delayed to the point of danger," in the surgeon general's opinion, the secretary of war on July 26, 1917, authorized the construction of temporary hospitals for Camp Fremont and the rest of the National Guard cantonments. On paper, they looked the same as any army hospital. "The important differences," writes a surgeon general's historian, "were that central heating, steam cooking, plumbing, sewerage, and interior lighting and ceiling, were not authorized...because of the intention to evacuate the troops from these camps before cold weather."[71]

Unfortunately, the mobilization did not occur as quickly as expected, and the winter of 1917–18 was an exceptionally bitter one in much of the United States. Conditions in the camps drew the anger of men's families, of the public at large and soon of Congress, which held hearings in the Senate Military Affairs Committee to discuss the slowness of mobilization and its effect on men's health. Pneumonia raged at New York's Camp Mills—the men called it "Camp Chills" and said it was so often flooded that "we found that our shoes would float"—and other eastern camps. Supply bottlenecks delayed cold-weather necessities such as blankets and wool shirts. Even at Camp Kearny outside San Diego, men complained of the cold winter nights.[72]

Some commentators felt that criticizing camp conditions was disloyal. As a character—a doctor, no less—in a *Collier's* short story put it, "Men have enlisted by the hundred thousand, willing to give their lives—for what? For an idea!...Which is the bigger fact, that, or that a few boys out of several hundred thousand had pneumonia in the camps? They would probably have had it anyway." Senator Hiram Johnson, a strong critic of the Wilson administration, led calls for these and later hearings. *Collier's* would soon demote him from "one of three senators who promise to raise the average" to one of "certain hot-headed congressional investigators." In December 1917, the army issued a general order allowing troops to wear civilian sweaters, provided that they were worn under regulation khaki and did not show. Women in communities across the country busied themselves knitting these sweaters. At Stanford, such duty was among the activities that female students could perform to satisfy the required war service that Wilbur asked of both men and women. In October and December 1917, War Secretary Baker authorized improvements to the camp hospitals, though Fremont's hospital, then still under construction, was not fully equipped with central steam heating until early 1919, when plans were afoot to make the hospital permanent under the auspices of the U.S. Public Health Service.[73]

Throughout the camp, buckets, barrels and small fire extinguishers provided the chief fire protection. Ten hose carts were allocated in 1917 to hook up to the camp's fire hydrants, but only four of them had wheels, and water pressure from the hydrants was low. Motorized fire engines, which carry pumps to boost water pressure, were then increasingly common in Bay Area communities but were not planned for the camps. Camp Fremont's hospital staff made particularly dogged attempts to improve fire protection. Like advocates of sewerage, they were stymied by army intentions that the camp be short-term. At least once in early 1918, water to the hospital ceased altogether in the middle of a medical procedure. Spring Valley, the vendor, installed a pump to increase pressure near the hospital but sought to remove it in June 1918 in favor of needs elsewhere. The hospital had no water tank to improve water pressure and storage and took its request for one all the way to the adjutant general in Washington, who denied it on March 23, 1918, "by order of the Secretary of War." In addition, hospital commander Colonel E.B. Frick fought budget reallocations in order to maintain a nighttime guard that could "insure [*sic*] the earliest discovery of fires." He tried an argument that the army might find more persuasive: "Prior to its establishment, immoral women gained access to [the] grounds." Eventually, the surgeon general found funds for a Camp Fremont fire station in a mid-1918 allocation for hospital improvements. But that was not until September 9, nearing the peak of fire season in California and too late to prevent the near-tragedy that followed.[74]

The hospital telephone operator on duty at 3:30 a.m. on September 13, 1918, Private First Class John T. Clark, noticed smoke coming through the wall near the ceiling of the switchboard room in the receiving ward of the hospital near the main entrance. He phoned the main camp and the Menlo Park Fire Department, which in each case entailed going through a civilian switchboard in Palo Alto, but the lines were out of order. (In a similar, fortunately minor, fire call that summer from a 319th Engineers kitchen, the Palo Alto operator was alleged to have been asleep.)

"I tried to get Camp Fremont several times, then ran down to K Ward and hollered, 'Fire,'" Clark told a board of inquiry convened later that morning. "The officer of the day says, 'Save the records.'" Clark did so and then, with the help of the night dispensary man, broke into the nearest clinic—the eye, ear, nose and throat clinic—and took out everything he could carry. They knew that medical equipment was in constant short supply. Others retrieved and connected the hose carts that Frick had persuaded his staff not to keep locked up against theft. Of the 950 patients on the grounds, those nearest to the fire were evacuated, with ambulatory men helping the bedridden ones. Evidence suggests that soldiers in the main camp were also roused to respond to this and other blazes. A Twelfth Infantry man writing several months after the event showed some confusion, since he got the hour and the weather but not the location right: "The one time when every man must be on his toes and ready to go regardless of circumstances is when fire call sounds…A gentle California autumnal rain was falling…Pistol shots rang out…Older men of the Regiment knew only too well what that meant."

In the infantryman's telling, it was "the old skating rink at Menlo Park, about half a mile from the camp proper," that had burned, but in any case, "Officers arrived a few minutes later and announced that the company would not be needed to help fight the fire as recall had already gone."[75]

Menlo Park's civilian engine had reached the hospital by 4:00 a.m., when Captain Potter, the fire marshal, arrived on the scene. Finding the fire under control with three hoses streaming water onto the remains of the receiving ward, he praised the "splendid cooperation" exhibited by all. Authorities in Washington approved the long-sought water tower within a week, an event hard to see as a coincidence.[76]

Less than three weeks later, however, danger returned to Camp Fremont. This time, it was lethal.

The 1918–19 influenza pandemic was one of the worst disasters ever to hit humanity, killing at least 50 million people worldwide, with an estimated 675,000 deaths in the United States alone. Military records show, in retrospect, how mass troop movements played a large part in spreading the flu around the world, from North America across the Atlantic and beyond and then back again. Some historians, in fact, locate the origins of the U.S. epidemic in army training camps in early 1918. A few troops from the army's Camp Funston (now Fort Riley), Kansas, are recorded as having contracted a mild, but highly contagious, strain of flu while home on leave in January and February 1918 in rural Haskell County and then bringing it back to the camp. "Flu needs a sizable population to keep it going, and the Haskell population was small," historian Sandra Opdycke noted. "Under normal circumstances the outbreak might have burned itself out right there." Instead, Funston's barracks and mess halls proved near-ideal media to propagate the virus, and the camp's siting at a rail junction helped to spread it far and wide. Other camps, including Fremont, noted similar bouts of flu that winter in their careful logging of health statistics, treating them as yet one more wave of the infectious disease so typical of the era. Historian Alfred Crosby notes that Harold W. Roberts's old unit, the Fifteenth Cavalry, suffered a suspicious wave of illness after leaving Camp Fremont for France in March 1918.[77]

However the virus got to Europe, it mutated and grew deadly. In late August, the *Journal of the American Medical Association* warned of a new "acute influenza-like disease" passing over the continent. Such warnings among the healthcare community were tempered by censorship from U.S. officials and dismissive, highly distorted coverage in the U.S. and global mass media. The epidemic coincided with the peak of U.S. military engagement on the Western Front. Concern over the disease coexisted in almost schizophrenic fashion with war-related mass meetings, parades, rallies for the Fourth Liberty Loan and other activities seemingly purpose-designed to spread it. On October 6, as the epidemic raged through the Bay Area, 150,000 people gathered in Golden Gate Park to file past a newsreel camera with messages of support for troops bound for the great Meuse-Argonne offensive that had commenced ten days earlier.

In 1918, almost nothing was known about viruses. An influenza diagnosis was based on its symptoms of sudden high fever and chills and then, in this new killer iteration, a blue tint on the ears and lips that spread to the

If You Think You Have INFLUENZA Send at Once for a DOCTOR

1. Don't worry
2. Go to bed
3. Take castor oil or salts
4. Keep comfortably warm
5. Take only milk and broth
6. Take no medicine but what the doctor orders
7. Cough or sneeze only into paper or old cloth and burn it up
8. Drink plenty of water
9. Stay abed until ordered up by the doctor
10. Remain in a well-ventilated room 2 or 3 days more

NATIONAL CHILD WELFARE ASSOCIATION
70 Fifth Avenue, New York

The epidemic coincided with the peak of U.S. mobilization to France. Health advice was hard to follow in the frenzied moment. *Menlo Park Historical Association.*

whole body as the virus attacked the patient's lungs and deprived him of oxygen. Many patients literally drowned as their lungs filled with bloody fluid. Others seemed to be recovering when they contracted a secondary pneumonia and died. The army directed its surgeons to take cultures from flu patients, living or dead, in hope of eventually finding a cause and a cure. It also called throughout the war for autopsies of soldiers who died in hospital, even though receiving autopsied bodies, with their marks and incisions, horrified the dead soldiers' next of kin. Various army personnel, from both the medical and quartermaster departments—the latter being responsible for transporting the bodies—begged the adjutant general in Washington for leniency in the practice. Camp Fremont's hospital commander was upbraided on September 26, 1918, by the acting surgeon general for not carrying out autopsies on enough of his patients. Only one patient had been autopsied in a previous month, the letter chides, and yet fifteen patients had died: "In every fatal case there is afforded the opportunity through autopsy to improve our methods of clinical diagnosis. Autopsies therefore tend to increase the efficiency of the hospital service, and hence are of military importance." The onslaught of patients in the fall of 1918 meant that such lab work was hardly carried out in a systematic manner. Only in isolated cases do 1918 flu samples survive. Yet the samples that do survive are very important, just as the army anticipated. In 2005, a team led by virologist Jeffery Taubenberger of the Armed Forces Institute of Pathology in Washington succeeded in mapping the complete 1918 flu genome from three samples. One was from an exhumed Alaskan, but two came from the autopsied lungs of army privates at Camp Jackson, South Carolina, and Camp Upton, New York, sectioned and preserved in tiny cubes of paraffin by harried army surgeons. Today, scientists inject the 1918 virus in mice and compare its deadly course with that of more recent flu strains in hope of learning what gave the 1918 virus its particular lethality.[78]

The first case at Camp Fremont of this new killer flu was reported on September 28, four days after the first known case in San Francisco. That day, the *Journal of the American Medical Association* appeared with a navy surgeon's report in Boston's overcrowded Commonwealth Pier barracks of what we now know as the mutated virus's stateside return. Word of the epidemic, of course, had traveled cross-country in advance of the scientific publication. On October 8, Camp Fremont's commander imposed a quarantine. It was tightened the following day to confine married officers to camp, for many had brought their families to Palo Alto. Comprehensive measures were imposed to enhance ventilation, as doctors had deduced that the horrifying new respiratory disease was probably airborne. Over the next six weeks, roughly 8,000 Camp Fremont troops, or roughly a quarter of the men in camp, were treated for respiratory diseases, 2,418 of whom were ill enough to be admitted to the base hospital. Pneumonia was diagnosed in 408 of the cases; of these, 147 died.[79]

Regimental commanders quickly relinquished the office space they had carved that spring from the planned regimental infirmaries. Twelfth Infantry commander Colonel Alfred Aloe moved his headquarters, with its battery of sixteen typewriters, from the infirmary space into the officers' clubhouse. "We rigged up a miniature hospital where at times we cared for almost 40 patients," one medic recalled. This way, he said, "there would be no danger of losing them when we left Camp Fremont," as would be the case if the sick were admitted to hospital. Even so, "Ambulances filled with masked patients left almost hourly for the Base Hospital." Aloe himself fell ill but recovered. At least four of the thirty-two sergeants and commissioned officers in the Twelfth's Headquarters Company fell ill as well. Extant camp documents do not say how Fremont's men were triaged, but elsewhere the decision was made by body temperature, with fevers of 101 degrees and above rating hospital care. All troops and visitors were stopped at the gate and questioned as to the necessity of their business in or out. The rule allowing troops to leave their unit areas and roam the camp freely on Wednesday afternoons and weekends was rescinded. The few men who left camp were expected to comply with local emergency laws such as the wearing of gauze masks; San Francisco and Palo Alto required them, while San Mateo County did not.[80]

In camp, ventilation became of prime importance. Men slept with their tent sides rolled up and their bunks alternating head to foot. Mess halls continued to operate, but all public gatherings were banned and all other activity moved outdoors. The YMCAs, Knights of Columbus huts, libraries and other recreational facilities so elaborately planned by the Commission on Training Camp Activities were all closed. Instead of browsing inside camp canteens for pies and other treats, men were served at the canteen door after queuing for hours outside. At the Twelfth Infantry chaplain's post, "now the only amusement place" for 3,500 men, one casualty was the tent where the well-loved regimental chaplains showed movies on a battered projector hauled to Camp Fremont from Regular Army service on the Mexican border. Not to be stopped, the padres screened their films *en plein air.* "The movie screen flapped like a sail in the night air," one infantryman remembered. "Only the precious old movie machine and Private Sherwood, the operator, were under the

Palo Alto, like many cities, required people to wear gauze masks in public in a failed attempt to quell the epidemic's spread. *Menlo Park Historical Association.*

shelter of a seven-by-nine." The chaplains were among very few Camp Fremont personnel who were allowed to freely cross the quarantine. This they did daily, to transfer letters—the Camp Fremont post office having evidently been overwhelmed or shut down—and other communications between the camp and the world outside. "We tried to look after things for you across the lines," one chaplain remembered of his daily trips to Palo Alto, his "pockets bulging" with money and documents collected in his role as "preacher, lawyer, banker, expressman, sport promoter, movie man, notary...to 3,500 men."[81]

Physicians had much less to give. The then-proprietary drug aspirin, which would have reduced patients' fevers, was available in America, the U.S. government having seized the U.S. patent of German firm A.G. Bayer when it expired in 1917. At the height of the epidemic, the surgeon general was recommending aspirin in high, even toxic, doses that were later implicated in their own spike of deaths. Still, the drug most mentioned in Camp Fremont records is, once again, narcotic. Morphine was given, according to the chief of the Army Medical Service, "to reduce the respiratory rate... thereby to prevent fatigue of the respiratory center." While doing nothing against fever, it would have eased the patients' pain. Nurses enforced total bed rest and administered cold wraps to reduce body temperature. Charles J. Sullivan, a Stanford member of the Student Army Training Corps who was treated for flu in the camp hospital, wrote to his fiancée that he survived by being "packed in ice two nights." Sullivan's descent into this horrifying new illness was characteristically sudden. On the afternoon of October 8, he was fretting to his girl that "fraternity life is smashed completely" by Stanford's militarization and that lack of army-issue boots was obliging him to march in his dress shoes. Hours later, he was carried from his dorm on a stretcher.[82]

Other Camp Fremont patients received treatments that could be judged as experimental. "Convalescent serum" was drawn from five patients and given to "five dangerously ill patients, all of whom were spitting blood." The results of the transfusions are not recorded. Because pneumonia was a better-known illness than the 1918 flu and, unlike the flu, had an identifiable pathogen, patients who lived long enough to develop secondary pneumonia received more heroic interventions. Four Camp Fremont patients received polyvalent antipneumococcus serum; three of them survived. Seventy patients received injections of the drugs coagulen and/or thromboplastin, presumably in hope of reducing fluid buildup in their lungs; of these patients, sixty recovered.[83]

Nurses had been in short supply throughout the war because they, unlike some other specialists, could not be trained quickly. The need was so dire, one source maintained, that some army officials seemingly overlooked the Wilson administration's segregationist policies and let up to 300 African American nurses "pass" into service in France. At army hospitals, full war strength was ascertained to be one nurse for ten beds. With the epidemic, the demand became far greater. In mid-October, with 164 patients critically ill at Camp Fremont and 25 nurses to care for them, the hospital chief appealed to Washington for more nurses, only to be told that "there is a greater emergency elsewhere." By this time, the army was offering contract nurses seventy-five dollars a month plus a four-dollar per diem, room and one ration a day, twice what it had offered at the start of the war. In the heat of the epidemic, however, nurses commanded whatever the market would bear. Rosalie Stern offered October 16 to pay the difference between army and private service to get nurses into Camp Fremont's wards and that same day obtained three nurses from Stanford. But she cautioned that "the Red Cross has no power…to compel a nurse to go where we wish."[84]

Against a disease for which physicians had no cure, patients credited intensive nursing care with saving their lives. Writing from Cot 25 on seventy-five-bed Ward L, Sullivan noted, "The nurses in this ward are 'at it' from six am until six at night and they are on 'double-quick' all the time…Regularly every hour one has a capsule (for variety two) or a thermometer or a glass of cough syrup or some vile tasting trash shoved into his face until he is worn out…the entire program right through the night." Rendered well enough to complain but not well enough to go home, Sullivan spent his days on the ward dodging nurses' bed-rest patrols in search of better letter-writing materials than the pencil and lined paper issued by the Knights of Columbus (for such were considered uncouth; a gentleman could be trusted to write indelibly and in a straight line) and for anything to read. The sole book he found on the ward

A Camp Fremont sergeant weathers the quarantine, which disrupted camp life but failed to halt the division's mobilization. *Menlo Park Historical Association, Hazel Rasor scrapbook.*

was an antiwar book, and one wonders whether it was among those on the banned list of the Commission on Training Camp Activities. "As it happens it deals vividly with war and the upsets caused by it with all the heartache and misgiving that it forces on individuals," Sullivan wrote to his fiancée. "I only feel more bitter against war as I see and prepare more for the actuality." The only civilian visitor or volunteer he saw in eight days was a priest, who gave him postage stamps and refused all payment.[85]

Military officials knew how well the flu traveled on trains and troop ships. Yet they refused to delay the mobilization with the need for men so grave. Camp Fremont soldiers recalled living these weeks in an agony of anticipation because they could almost taste being in the Big Show. They regarded the flu and the quarantine as roadblocks to their imminent deployment. Quarantine magnified the frustration they already felt when they saw five thousand of their campmates leave in August for Siberia or when they stood by all that summer as units in other camps deployed to France.

Bored and wanting only to see action, some Fremont men viewed quarantine as a rule to be honored in the breach. "These are times when he feels like kicking over the traces altogether and going AWOL," an infantryman remembered. "Only a few sentries are between him and the Big Village and it is not hard to slip through the line on a dark night." He might be court-martialed, this soldier admitted, but frankly, quarantine and the "mill," or stockade, felt much the same. Further, while quarantine was at best an annoyance, "there are some who are of the conviction that a man cannot claim to have been a good soldier unless he has done a turn in the mill." The Twelfth Infantry chaplains phrased the quarantine as a sacrifice that men could make toward a better body politic, saying that "the confinement brought to all of us more knowledge of each other and more friendliness" and an "appreciation of the spirit of self-control, of service and of brotherhood."[86]

Still, the chaplains assisted in some of the quarantine's subversions. They seem to have interpreted their mission as guarding the greater health of the men—a health that included social interactions. Often, this was to help a soldier get married. Chaplain Lieutenant Donald T. Grey of the Twelfth had the help of a sympathetic San Mateo County official for one nuptial:

> *The girl was from Washington state with her mother. The General would not let the soldier out—only to the edge of camp. Both parties have to be present before the County Clerk, and to sign the "big book," which had*

> *never been outside the County Clerk's office, not since the Spaniards ruled in the land...But the girl was pretty, and maybe she used the feminine last resort, for she telephoned that if the Chaplain and the soldier would be in front of Camp HQ at 11 a.m, the clerk would bring down the big book... The sun had broken through, the clerk and his deputy had arrived, and on the counter of the Andrus Bus Station* [between Menlo Park and the camp] *lay the big book...Whirling around the Clerk said, "Now go to it, chaplain"...Out on the grass under the nearest oak, the Chaplain read the service. Half an hour later he found them down by the Hostess House enjoying their honeymoon two paces apart.*[87]

For Nancy Bristow, the quarantine was a literal and blatant expression of progressivism's power to coerce the individual in the service of the public good. Bristow sees in resistance to the 1918 flu quarantine and other public health measures, such as masking, an early sign of the fatigue with progressivism that emerged after the war: "As the epidemic waned, so, too, did Americans' willingness to accept governmental intervention in their daily lives." The Camp Fremont men's escapades seem expressions of youthful vigor, a drive to experience life amid the prospect of imminent death. Having emerged intact, survivors congratulated themselves on embodying the values of "fraternalism, health and vigor" that they said helped win the war. As for flu deaths, Camp Fremont's men offered them as evidence that the division had offered the ultimate sacrifice despite not seeing combat. They valorized their flu dead as war dead. The survivors, even if they did not fight a human foe, had triumphed over the unseen enemy that was the epidemic. They had become tough enough, they told themselves, to scare the Kaiser into capitulation. These qualities, wrote Lieutenant Clifton R. Gordon of the Twelfth, would serve after the war to make them a "great leavening influence for public and private good, each one of them a better citizen for the experiences he has undergone." Quarantine, with all its unpleasantness, had helped to make that so.[88]

In fact, the quarantine did not stop the mobilization. The bulk of Camp Fremont's Eighth Division, including the Twelfth Infantry, was mobilized while the camp quarantine was in effect, receiving its orders on October 10 and boarding the first trains for the East Coast eight days later. The men of the Twelfth crossed the continent in rail cars with windows wide open to reduce contagion. "After you're as cold as you can get you can't take cold," one infantryman reasoned. Nonetheless, Benedict Crowell's official war history observes that "many a man was taken from the trains of the Eighth Division to hospitals along the route, and many a one who entrained at Camp Fremont was dead before his comrades saw the Manhattan skyline." Another Twelfth Infantry chaplain, Lieutenant Eugene B. Carroll, braved daily contagion across Camp Fremont's quarantine line only to contract influenza en route to the Atlantic embarkation, dying on November 21, 1918. The Twelfth memorialized him as one of thirty-three members who sacrificed their lives in war service. The rest detrained in Camp Mills—still chilly, by their reports—where, according to a brigade commander, they stayed "under the most miserable conditions of rain and cold without adequate facilities for their comfort." Some men in the regiment came so close to sailing to France that their baggage had actually been put aboard troop transports when news came of the Armistice and the trip was canceled. Camp Fremont's quarantine was not lifted until November 16, by which time only a couple of thousand troops, mostly depot workers and hospital staff and patients, remained in camp.[89]

The official fatality rate at Camp Fremont, according to the chief of the Army Medical Service in Los Angeles, was 36 percent of pneumonia patients and 5 percent for the epidemic overall. These official statistics include only men admitted to hospital and not those treated in camp. Also uncounted were men in Camp Fremont units who became ill in other camps after mobilization, whether they left before the quarantine (including the 319th Engineers) or in the midst of it (including the 12th Infantry). In each case, these men traveled into the path of the epidemic as they moved toward the war.[90]

Camp Fremont's 319th Engineers were mobilized in mid-September, a month ahead of the 12th Infantry and most of the 8th Division. The men harbored the great hope that they would finally use their training as pioneers, as sappers—those intrepid builders of trenches, firing posts and other structures used by combat troops on the Western Front. The deadly fall epidemic had not yet reached California when the engineers entrained for Camp Upton, New York, an embarkation point for the Atlantic voyage. But, as Crosby notes, it had reached Camp Upton, and on September 24, when the men of the 319th boarded the HMT *Briton*, a former South African mail packet on which they made up the great majority of the passengers, influenza sailed with them.

Many remembered the early days of the crossing as joyful. They sailed from New York in a convoy of some fifteen ships, escorted at the

Crowding on troop transports raised the epidemic's toll. This cartoonist makes the best of it. *From* The Twelfth U.S. Infantry—Its Story by Its Men.

outset by destroyers, a battleship, a submarine chaser, a dirigible and two airplanes—fully protected, one officer of the 319th recalled, "on all sides and overhead." Lifeboat drills were held daily, and the life jackets donned until further orders enhanced the feeling of protection. A few days out to sea, however, events turned ugly. A storm arose that was to persist until the crossing's end, and the troops, confined by the weather, began to fall ill. Within two or three days, some two hundred men were sick enough to require hospitalization in quarters that were soon overflowing. The sick men were moved to the promenade deck, despite half-gale winds, to isolate them from the healthy on the decks below.[91]

A private, Robert James Wallace, later told Crosby that he fought this consignment to the elements. "Suit yourself," snapped the doctor. "You have a temperature of 103. You are sick. If you want to go below and infect all of them down there, go ahead." On deck, wrapped in his overcoat and only blanket, Wallace lay febrile as his other gear blew overboard. He drifted, Crosby writes, into "a delirious fantasy about a great rope of colored silk down which he could slide into peace and quiet—but *mustn't*, because that would be *desertion*." Sick officers were allowed to remain in their cabins. Lieutenant Watson B. Joyes of E Company watched helplessly as his friend and bunkmate began to die. "Toward the last [he] realized that he was not going to pull through," Joyes wrote the dead man's family in Kentucky. "I know he fought hard, for I was with him on the boat and slept in the same room."[92]

Soon the smoking rooms, the library and even the stair landings of the *Briton* were paved with sick men. A contingent of navy nurses fortuitously had come aboard at the last minute, and these were credited with keeping the death toll low. Still, at least six men and two officers of the 319th died, as did one of the nurses. "You read about funerals at sea and think it might be interesting to witness one, but after having so buried six of your comrades you feel you have had enough," another E Company lieutenant remembered. The weather was so bad and the troops so ill that men attending one such funeral could not stand upright unassisted. "The pallbearers brought the body draped in the National Colors…between a double line of F Company men clinging to the rigging or each other to maintain a footing, but all came to the right-hand salute as their comrade passed," a captain recalled. Up and down the convoy, the raising and lowering of flags on masts indicated similar burials from other ships. The storm worsened on the final night. Men well enough to notice their surroundings did not learn until landing on October 7 that another ship in the convoy, the *Otranto*, had collided with yet another transport, the *Kashmir*, and run aground on the Isle of Islay off the Scottish coast, breaking nearly in half and losing more than four hundred people aboard.[93]

The regiment left a trail of sick men across England and western France. Many would recover in hospitals and catch up later, but one officer wrote that at least 15 of the 319th Engineers survived the *Briton* voyage only to die in Liverpool. Overall, Crosby writes, 6.43 percent of transported men who developed flu and/or pneumonia on Atlantic crossings in September and October 1918 died before landing or within a few days afterward. This was a higher mortality rate than that of Fremont or other stateside army camps, where healthy men and minor cases could be more effectively sequestered. The *Leviathan*, which landed at Brest the day the *Briton* landed at Liverpool, carried 9,000 soldiers, of whom some 2,000 became ill, 969 required hospitalization upon landing and up to 90 died on board. In mid-October, army chief of staff Peyton March agreed to reduce what he called "the packing-in process" on troop ships by 10 percent, but that was all. March insisted to Wilson that men were vetted for health before embarkation and that, as Crosby writes, "the

The 319th Engineers smuggled Monty the bear to France in a drum case of their regimental band. *Menlo Park Historical Association.*

lives lost to influenza must be balanced against those which could be saved if the war could be brought to a speedy end."[94]

Private Wallace resisted becoming this kind of shrinkage. He told Crosby he didn't want to go to hospital, because people died there. Rain, mud and lack of supplies or medical attention at the debarkation camp outside Liverpool persuaded Wallace to take matters into his own hands. He "sneaked off and found illicit shelter in an Army cookhouse, where an Italian-American let him sit by one of the stoves" until his secondary infection broke, "found him a cap and a mess kit, and fed him stewed apricots," along with "brusque comments on the ways a soldier can survive when the going gets rough." Rejoining his unit after three days AWOL, Wallace told Crosby that no one had noticed he was gone.[95]

Meanwhile, Colonel Curtis Otwell, the 319th's commander, had also fallen ill and was left to convalesce in Romsey, the regiment's next stop after Liverpool. His engineers reached Le Havre without him and learned, to their dismay, that they would not be sappers after all. As Lieutenant August L. Barreau remembered:

> *You want to hear the big guns, you are eager to get into the big game, to get at last the fulfillment of your wish toward which you have worked ever since the war began. It is no cheerful news to hear...that you are bound for Brest, about as far from the front as France will allow you to go. Spirits sink another few notches on finding out that you are to work on barrack buildings, under orders from officers of a Services of Supply organization, your most able Colonel being in England on account of sickness.*[96]

When the engineers got to Brest on October 16, the scale of the AEF operation there astonished them. "It is difficult to conceive the enormity of material," another lieutenant wrote. "War material. Warehouses strung out as far as you could see, stuffed with supplies. Upon inquiry as to where it could all have come from, you were informed: America." Their new mission at Base Section No. 5 was to help build out Old Pontanezen Barracks into a rest camp for 155,000 men, complete with plumbing, electricity, water, roads and sewerage. They were sobered to realize that the facilities they had traveled six thousand miles to build would be larger, more comfortable and engineered to a higher standard than anything they themselves had encountered in army service, either in Europe or stateside at Camp Fremont. One officer noted that he could more easily get an extra blanket, if needed, at Brest than he could at Camp Fremont. While the latter had

Colonel Curtis W. Otwell, commander of the 319th Engineers, caught influenza en route to France. He recovered and lived in Palo Alto into his eighties. *Menlo Park Historical Association.*

been conceived for a temporary occupation that dragged on for months, the AEF, less than a month from the end of the war, was now digging in for a long stay. Every component had been hauled, like the engineers themselves, at great risk and cost across the Atlantic. "Now you think of blankets, two extra blankets are not many, but two and more for two million men are, and blankets are only one item on the list of equipment," one officer mused. "Then you must reflect back to America...what a small part of the whole it was."[97]

The 319th major who became field engineer at Pontanezen was told it was a priority job "because of the many deaths that had occurred at Brest because of lack of shelter." He wrote, "The men were appealed to." This appeal took the form of a competition among his units for barracks per day erected. In part, this barracks-building competition was a trick of psychology, meant to take the men's minds off their disappointment at not being sent to the front. The engineers' B Company also tackled Base Section No. 5's new kitchens and mess halls, each large enough for nearly two infantry regiments, or six thousand men.[98]

The men were energized, not depersonalized, at the magnitude of their task. They saw themselves not as cogs in wheels but as skilled and efficient workers. They were also very competitive. While higher-ups had set a benchmark of ten buildings per regiment per day (the major apparently revised this upward to thirteen), the Camp Fremont men managed to erect up to thirty. Their buildings went up "like mushrooms." A sick second lieutenant hospitalized for two weeks at Brest "on returning to duty was stunned by the sight of hundreds of barrack buildings, bath houses, kitchens and latrines where none had been before."[99]

The engineers saw their work as benefiting other soldiers. In their minds, they rephrased their failure to reach the front and the drudgery of their duties as a sacrifice, a strategic retreat from hard-fought objectives to put others more fortunate over the top. The hard crossing, the epidemic and the discomfort en route also were rephrased as sacrifice and, "since we were unable to do our bit in supreme sacrifice," as incentive to provide for others "comforts that they have not known for months," comforts that had been denied them.[100]

The barracks-building competition in Base Section No. 5, we are told, was won by the 319th's D Company. Its reward was to be sent on detached service to prepare surveys for a ten-thousand-bed hospital near Evreaux for the wounded who were expected to flow in from the front.

An officer in B Company also initially interpreted his new orders as a reward. "You get orders to move to a little town called Beaune," he wrote. "You are envied by the entire regiment. You think you will get in the big fight, but are fooled." Instead, B Company was also assigned to build a hospital. Unlike the hospital that the engineers left behind at Camp Fremont, it was to be of concrete. It was therefore to be fire-resistant, unlike Camp Fremont's hospital, where hundreds of patients remained incapacitated that month with influenza and pneumonia. It was to have "modern plumbing and electric lights, with a complete water and sewerage system," the officer recalled. The

319th Engineers got to work, having weathered the harsh passage, influenza, half-gale-force winds, the shipwreck of a sister vessel and a slog through rain to poorly equipped rest camps to arrive at this mission of providing other men comfort. Meanwhile, the Armistice was signed in the days intervening between the events and the officers' writing about them. The Evreaux survey was called off, but the Beaune hospital was not. As Lieutenant Joyes saw it: "The war is over but the wounded and sick must still be cared for."[101]

Chapter 5

MAPPING THE FUTURE

How World War I Helped Shape the West

Most Americans measured their contribution to World War I by what they gave up for it. They used the language of sacrifice to derive meaning from a conflict that for most was distant and relatively brief. While the front and its industrial carnage were almost unimaginably far away, sacrifice of any kind seemed personal and immediate. The American Red Cross enrolled thirty-one million members in 1918, including eleven million children, who pledged to serve the war effort in ways large and small. More than half of America's four million men under arms, including Camp Fremont's 8th Division, failed to see battle before peace broke out. Many phrased their failure to attain martial glory as a similar sacrifice. They built barracks and patrolled docks and sublimated their disappointment into pride in their military discipline. As the 319th Engineers' Lieutenant August L. Barreau wrote, "You never forgot that though being skilled engineers you were soldiers first."[102]

Roughly 116,000 Americans made the supreme sacrifice, dying in action or from influenza or other disease while in service. After the war, Americans mourned these dead with memorials raised by public subscription all over the country. Stanford's Ray Lyman Wilbur sat on the national panel that set guidelines for these memorials: that they be buildings and that they be serviceable, such as auditoriums. From these guidelines emerged the hundreds of Veterans Memorial Buildings from the 1920s and 1930s that still dot America's campuses, county seats and civic centers. In creating places for people to gather, ideally for the public good, these memorials spatialize and carry forward the service and sacrifice of people like tank driver Harold W. Roberts and driver and aviator Arthur Kimber.

Another legacy of the war is even more pervasive and practical. It resides in the skills many soldiers learned in such wartime tasks as creating Camp Fremont's munitions ranges. The engineers who planned and mapped Camp Fremont became construction supervisors, mappers and petroleum engineers, all building on their army experience. These citizen-soldiers were poised to develop the West as the automobile transformed life and the landscape in the 1920s and 1930s. Their legacy hides in plain sight, embedded in the growth that now all but obliterates Camp Fremont's physical traces.

Initially, Fremont's 319th Engineers interpreted their war service in the prevalent self-sacrificing terms, proving their worth by following unwelcome orders as a soldier should. Yet a map the engineers made of Camp Fremont's trench maneuver ground for divisional war games in early August 1918 illustrates how they would have preferred their role, and America's role, to be remembered. In its trenches grandly named for great U.S. battles, the engineers' map taps the romantic symbolism that the government used to sell the war to the men meant to fill the trenches. In its technical features new to America but standard in Europe—the metric system and Lambert cartographic projection, adopted to improve the accuracy of Allied artillery fire—the map shows how army training would give some men opportunities to become exceptional. Meanwhile, the features the map depicts were backfilled by Stanford in the 1940s, occasionally to emerge as sinkholes after heavy rains as a palimpsest of the Peninsula's days of war.

Camp Fremont's 960-acre trench maneuver ground occupied the site of today's SLAC (Stanford Linear Accelerator Center) National Laboratory and adjacent property, bordered on the northwest by Sand Hill Road. Its hundreds of yards of trenches, dugouts and subterranean galleries were laid out by the 319th Engineers from March through August 1918. They were used by regiments during that time as well as in the 8th Division's larger games on August 9–10. All World War I training camps were supposed to have trench fields to acquaint men with Western Front warfare, but Camp Fremont's appears to have been unusually elaborate. This was partly because Stanford's extensive grounds and favorable geology made more land available for such a project and partly, a 319th captain noted, because "new and interesting experiments" were needed "to hold in check the impatience for active service" in men growing restless as troops in other

Student Army Training Corps on maneuvers. The anachronistic close formation taught in the army made men vulnerable to machine gun attack. *Stanford University Archives.*

camps throughout the country deployed to France. One man of the 319th was killed and several badly injured while dynamiting a trench dugout into the Stanford foothills late one night in mid-June 1918. Archaeological and documentary evidence—including a 2010 magnetometric survey of features on the system's periphery and photos taken of the galleries circa 1940 by spelunking boys—attests to the trench field's postwar survival. How closely it corresponded to what is on the map is hard to determine today because the War Department only declassified the map in 1946, after Stanford had sealed the galleries. SLAC's construction in the early 1960s further disturbed the ground.[103]

The Camp Fremont map depicts three lines of trenches as they would be dug in actual Western Front battle: a front line, a support line and a rear line, with communication passages perpendicular to and linking the main battle trenches. These passages zigzagged to thwart enemy enfilade fire and to contain damage from shelling, and at Camp Fremont they were called by the French term *boyau*, which means "guts." All the trenches are named, as they would be on a real battlefield. They face coastward, metaphorically expressing Manifest Destiny but in reality directing live ordnance away from the university, Menlo Park and Palo Alto. A gun emplacement just beyond what is now the Stanford Hills subdivision faces coastward as well, toward the artillery range. It was meant to support long-range guns firing from behind the trenches into putative enemy territory on and around Richard Hotaling's cattle pastures off Arastradero Road.

Members of the Twelfth Infantry remembered, not fondly, marching up Sand Hill Road in gas masks to take and retake the trenches and their surrounding hills:

> *Finally the Stanford crossroads, long prayed for, would appear through the dense fog on the portion of the right goggle which we were able to see out of, and life would be worth living once more. We would clean the slobber off our blouses, our overalls and our faces, stack arms along the board fence, and fall out for a moment of recuperation…* [until] *bloodless warfare commenced anew. On hill 438 the bombers of L Co. could be seen hurtling Mark 1s* [grenades] *into Strassburg Boyeau* [sic], *while on hill 500 K Company could be seen consolidating the crest… All the hills were alive with the wearers of cheesecloth hatbands of many hues. If Private Jones wore a red hatband, he had to imagine his pockets laden down with bombs, but if this were changed to blue, he had to remember that he was the operator of a Browning automatic, and conduct himself accordingly.*[104]

Troops marched in gas masks from their Camp Fremont quarters to the trench ground on Sand Hill Road. *Menlo Park Historical Association.*

If this infantryman, writing some months after the fact, failed to get the trench name exactly right, it was probably because he did not receive a map. World War I infantrymen were generally not issued maps, but instead found a place in the line where their commanding officers told them to go. Maps were the purview of officers and the technical specialists who used them to plot artillery fire against distant, unseen targets. In fact, like the Camp Fremont trench map, maps were often classified. Maps borne by messenger, historian John Keegan writes, were the only reliable way a commander behind the lines could receive accurate information in an era when firepower and troop strength vastly overshadowed the capacity of long-distance communication to direct these assets. Camp Fremont's war games featured one portentous advantage that the troops of the future Silicon Valley had over peers in Europe: they had a portable two-way radio, donated by Cecelia Casserly of Burlingame and probably built by the Federal Wireless Company of Palo Alto. It took five men to carry and thirty-eight seconds to set up, but it worked. Instead, Western Front commanders from platoon level upward relied on maps that by September 1918 were updated daily on corps of engineers presses so as to direct the coming night's bombardments, a total of 309,000 sheets printed for the AEF's St. Mihiel offensive alone.[105]

Americans in the ranks flocked to what little army map training was offered, in part because they foresaw its tremendous potential in later civilian life as urban growth, new highways and the rise of the automobile augured new uses and markets. One private, denied a slot in a map training course, sought to instruct himself by sketching clandestine maps of camp that he mailed home to avoid detection and military discipline. The War Department's shortchanging of map work in favor of close-order drill, bayonet training and other outmoded subjects aligns with "systemic problems associated with the nation's lack of preparation" that Richard Faulkner identifies as contributing to the AEF's poor training, particularly of junior officers. One German commander wrote that "walking around noisily with unfolded maps" made American officers easy targets for snipers.[106]

Camp Fremont's trench map, like others, therefore, depicts a world designed and mapped by relative elites in which private soldiers had to find their way. Its trench names functioned as street names, for direction. A rich lore has arisen around World War I trench names, particularly the British trench names like "Rats Alley" and "Piccadilly Trench," that, according to British map scholar Peter Chasseaud, lent "a comforting, if illusory, element" of home, safety or morale-lifting humor to a "lethal, dirty and uncomfortable reality." The French, in contrast, named their trenches for

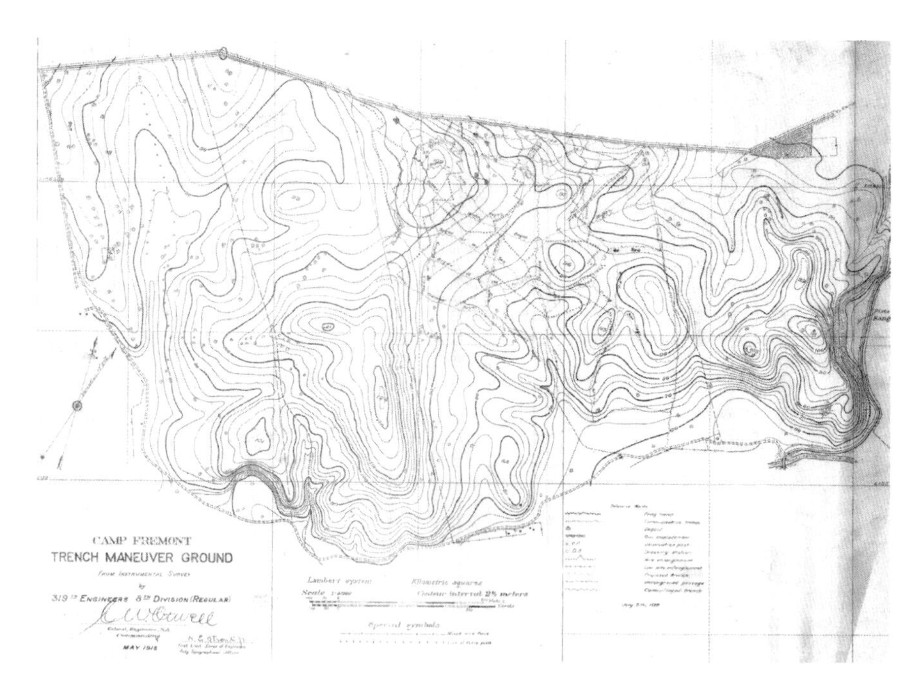

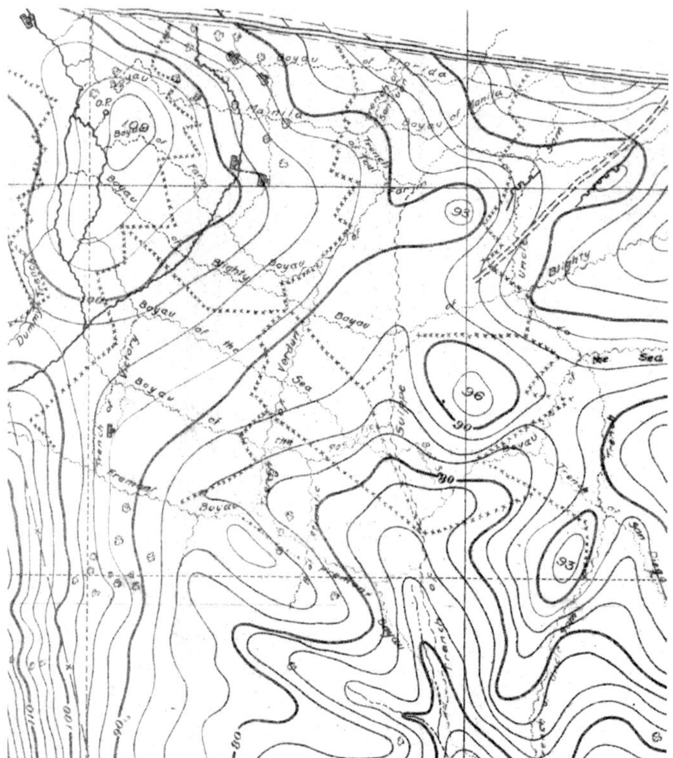

The 319th planned and mapped Camp Fremont's trench ground off Sand Hill Road. Its dugouts occasionally emerge as sinkholes after heavy rains. *National Archives.*

inspirational value, after great French heroes and battles. Camp Fremont's trench map is American, but its French influence shows not just in many of its names but also in its cartographic style, which the 319th mastered in early 1918 by copying French models. The victories this map cites are great American victories, redolent of the *fin-de-siècle* dash and romanticism that America's shapers of culture carried forward to glamorize this new and very different war.[107]

There is a Boyau of Manila, after America's Battle of Manila Bay in the Philippines. There's a Trench of San Juan Hill, after the charge by Teddy Roosevelt and his Rough Riders in the Spanish-American War. Other names honor French spots to which Americans were then deploying or had already made their mark, as Camp Fremont's soldiers stood by all summer and looked impotently on. There's a Trench of Toul, after the AEF's Second Army headquarters outside a walled fortress town much like Verdun but forty miles southeast. A Trench of Suippe may honor the village where, a day after Lincoln's birthday in 1918, U.S. artillerymen embedded with the Fourth French Army made headlines by becoming the first Yanks to fire a large-caliber rail gun in the war. Conspicuously missing from Camp Fremont's trench map are battles that pitted American against American: no Indian battles, no Civil War battles, even though some of the Regular Army units actually present at Camp Fremont had distinguished themselves at Gettysburg and, according to their own histories, had spent much of the intervening five decades breaking strikes in industrial cities and subduing Modocs, Apaches and other Native American tribes. Rather, the map expresses the unity that the army aimed to forge—as one Twelfth Infantry man put it, the "one in all and all in one."

By June 1918, as Camp Fremont's 319th Engineers laid out and mapped their practice Trench of Toul, the AEF's First Division had already been training for months near the real Toul. On June 8, while their counterparts in France prepared to enter the war, the men of Camp Fremont trooped in to a patriotic song festival at Stanford Stadium attended by California Governor George Stephens and fifteen thousand civilian spectators. Singing, the War Department held, developed a man's chest and lungs, and singing in close-order drill furthered unit cohesion. Having inducted an assistant conductor of the San Francisco Symphony, the 319th Engineers won the event with their rendition of the Soldiers' Chorus from Gounod's *Faust*, its refrain altered to "Skilled men who smile at a coward's fears/One hundred per cent, the Engineers!" The Austrian American contralto Ernestine Schumann-Heink presented the victor's trophy, her presence inspiring

Colonel Otwell leads the 319th to victory in the Patriotic Song Festival on June 9, 1918, with an adapted "Soldiers' Chorus" from Gounod's *Faust*. *Stanford University Archives.*

particular pathos because she had one son in the German navy and three others on the American side.

None of this was fighting, or even particularly useful preparation for fighting. The close-order formations that troops learned in such exercises made it that much easier for enemy machine guns to mow them down. Sentiment obscured the lack of preparation, just as it tinted the portrayal of combat. Nine days after the festival, Private Henry B. Nelson of the 319th lay dead, and several other engineers gravely injured, when their dynamite went off too early as they bombed a trench-field dugout into the Ladera sandstone. They had been working at night, apparently to simulate battlefield conditions. It was the closest any of the 319th Engineers would get to a heroic battle death, though at least two dozen died of disease in camp or en route to France. Certainly, it was a sacrifice to be honored. Yet the engineers, in their many surviving letters and reunion notes stretching into the 1970s, never mention Nelson's death in those terms. By then, the engineers had reaped years of advantages that their army training gave them. They had built highways, led technical institutes and university science departments, created an island in San Francisco Bay. They had no more need to validate themselves through the rhetoric of sacrifice. When they mentioned Nelson's death in later years, they only mentioned fear and pain. Camp Fremont's map reflects their hopes as younger men as they waited in 1918—a desire for

FOR THE BOYS AT CAMP FREMONT

Mammoth Patriotic
Song Festival

PROGRAM

SCHUMANN-HEINK

World's Greatest Contralto

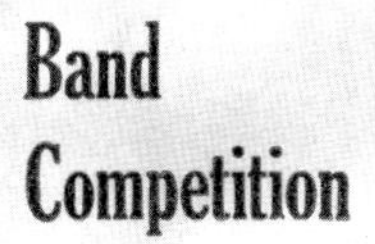

Band
Competition

Military
Pageant

Chorus of
10,000
Soldiers

Chorus of
10,000
Soldiers

Greatest Open Air Concert Ever Held
in America

THE ENTIRE FESTIVAL IS UNDER
THE PERSONAL SUPERVISION OF

FESTYN DAVIES

Musical Director of Camp Fremont

Stanford Stadium
Palo Alto

Sunday, June 9th
at 2 p. m.

The festival kept troops busy while raising funds for their recreation and for civilian war workers in France. *Menlo Park Historical Association.*

valor that they prayed would not elude them. They envisioned a continuum of past and future U.S. victories, symbolically linked the way the trenches are linked on the 319th Engineers' map.

Yet the map's ultimate importance is not symbolic but material, for it posed challenges and incorporated innovations that men like the 319th Engineers would ultimately use to transform the American landscape. Within weeks in early 1918, the army obliged its engineers to become proficient in the metric system used in Europe, as well as the newly adopted Lambert conformal conic map projection that improved the accuracy of artillery fire on the Western Front. This forward-looking assignment, unlike the close-order drill and bayonet work that filled so much of the army training schedule, had immediate application both in the war and in civil society. Camp Fremont's trench map is an early example of the modern mapping that would be adopted after the war by the U.S. Geological Survey and Coast and Geodetic Survey, the nation's official mappers, and thus would underlie all levels of land-use planning.

As well as helping to direct troop movements on widening and deepening fronts, maps became critical in twentieth-century warfare because they were used to plot artillery fire. Artillerymen used trigonometry to plot firing points from ever more powerful guns to unseen and ever more distant positions, calculating an angle from weapon to observer in a forward post to target. The culminations of this trend were both German: the feared Paris Gun, which shot seventy-five miles over the Allied lines into the city, and the "fire waltz" that choreographed various gases and shells into parts of the line where their particular qualities would have the most lethal effect. Both sides employed another innovation of World War I battle, the "creeping barrage" of artillery fire that covered infantrymen moving from their trenches toward an enemy position. Gunners needed very accurate bearings to avoid hitting their own troops during these movements. They sought maps that would allow them to direct fire within fifteen yards of accuracy on either side, which was most guns' margin of error. When America entered the war, it did not yet have maps with the accuracy and modernity being developed in Europe. Maps before the spring of 1918 characterize Camp Fremont and vicinity not only in English measurement but also often in such archaic measures as "chains."

The Lambert conformal conic projection of Camp Fremont's map was invented in 1772 but first used by the French in the war in late 1915. It conceives of a map as a cone seated vertically onto the sphere of the earth, with the earth's features projected onto the cone's surface. The place where this hypothetical cone touches the earth is where the map conforms most closely to what it represents, and this line becomes the reference parallel to which the rest of the map is scaled. All two-dimensional maps of a three-dimensional object necessarily have some distortion, but a Lambert map is extremely accurate from east to west, which is, on the Western Front, the general direction that the action went. Starting in December 1915, the French gradually replaced their earlier Bonne map projection, which could not be accurately scaled or extended eastward, with the new Lambert maps. French artillery on the Somme used older maps, whose significant east–west distortion Chasseaud argues helped to misdirect the fire, while Lambert maps arrived in time to help conclude the ten-month French effort at Verdun.

The U.S. Army directed its engineers and artillerymen to convert to the metric system on the rather late date of January 4, 1918. On February 1, it adopted the Lambert system and began publishing coordinates for use in making maps. On February 11, the 319th was given a French map of Gondrecourt, one of the first AEF training sites; told to copy it for instructional purposes; and ordered to lay out and map the Stanford trench maneuver ground using the new systems. By May, the engineers had plotted both that map and a larger one of Camp Fremont's newly acquired artillery range in the hills behind campus. It probably helped that the chief topographical officer, Lieutenant Henry C. Strout, was an MIT graduate. The average army inductee had 6.8 years of schooling, while more than a third of the 319th were high school graduates and one in nine had attended college.

It's remarkable that the army did not order its mappers and artillerymen to go metric until 1918, considering that upon landing they would be thrust into a metric war. Yet Camp Lewis, in Tacoma, addressed the problem even later. Its commanding general sought fifty copies of the engineers' Gondrecourt map on September 30, 1918, to help train his own specialists. Camp Fremont's commander had to decline; his engineers had already sailed. For most men in the ranks, up-to-date training was delayed even further or did not come at all. The U.S. Department of Commerce, which regulates weights and measures, did not issue metric teaching aids for infantrymen until the fall of 1918, when nearly two million troops were already in France. Camp Fremont received these booklets on October 30, 1918, when most of the Eighth Division had already left California. The commander gave the booklets to the Camp Fremont surgeon, to edify hospital patients and staff.

Metrication failed to conquer America, to be sure. Yet the rigor and confidence needed to switch quickly to the metric system, considering that lives in battle would depend on how accurately their maps were drawn, is the type of benefit the engineers said helped them for the rest of their lives. More than the progressivism-inflected mass singing and moral instruction that the War Department used to forge its crucible of soldiery, this specific technical training really did confer advantages on the few men privileged to receive it. It contributed to the engineers' feeling that they were not cogs in wheels but exceptional. While they may have seen their duties as mundane in 1918, they later appreciated the opportunity they were given and the watershed moment in American history in which it came.

The engineers returned to the United States on August 27, 1919, "their enthusiasm aged and tempered, but still present," Major Dorst remembered. The work at Brest had only added to their skills, and the men knew this. "The 'Battle of Brest' was an adventure filled with educating problems," Captain Herbert Taylor wrote. "Problems of modern municipal construction were met in every phase of the work." Most important was the men's facility in embracing challenge and change.[108]

Major Dorst stayed with the Army Corps of Engineers and built projects in service of the much larger World War II mobilization that, like Camp Fremont, contributed directly or indirectly to U.S. expansion and development. As district engineer for San Francisco, Dorst was in charge of dredging man-made Treasure Island into San Francisco Bay. Another captain who stayed with the corps, Fremont E. Roper, supervised construction of the 1,700-mile AlCan Highway connecting the then-territory of Alaska with the contiguous United States. In its first iteration, completed in 1942, this rough but strategic road crossed streams via pontoon bridges like those that the 319th had practiced building in 1918 at Felt Lake in the Stanford hills. Other 319th veterans helped to build California's highway system and the San Francisco–Oakland Bay Bridge. Some worked for Standard Oil, other petrochemical extractors or mining companies. Otwell supervised an early study for the Bay Bridge, when Hunters Point was being considered for its San Francisco terminus. Working for California Lands, a holding company of the Bank of America, he was consulting engineer for Union Station in downtown Los Angeles. Captain Taylor became dean of the Worcester Technical School in Massachusetts. Private Maxwell Short, who lost both legs in the June 1918 trench-field dynamite accident, went on to get a Harvard PhD and ultimately to chair the department of geology and mineralogy at the University of Arizona. "The accident changed Short's life, but in making adjustments to new conditions he contributed greatly to geology in fields he probably otherwise would not have pursued," one colleague noted. The rare North American mineral shortite is named for him.[109]

Others from the 319th became real estate agents and developers. Many of the maps they used in their projects derived ultimately from the popular USGS 7½-minute 1:24,000 topographic maps made after the war by army-trained mappers and surveyors using the Lambert projection pioneered in the Bay Area by Camp Fremont's engineers. In the months after the Armistice, many army engineers and technical specialists fulfilled their military service by surveying and drafting such maps for the USGS and Coast and Geodetic Survey. They worked alongside survey personnel who had assisted with AEF mapmaking in France. These maps, usually dated 1918–20, often bear a War Department credit. Often, the metric stick on these maps is larger than the English stick, reversing customary USGS practice, as if the makers of the map wore metrication as a badge of service. The maps use the Lambert projection in thirty-four states, mostly those that run predominantly east to west. An exception is California, which is longer north to south but was mapped using Lambert in seven east–west zones. Maxwell Short was among the veterans who taught this topographic mapping, first at the USGS and later as a volunteer instructor for troops during World War II. The maps, at first often almost bare of human settlement, were updated as the population grew. The engineers were not spreading progressivism the ideology, which disillusioned many people in the postwar era. Rather, they spread material progress, which energized people and seemed more useful. Relics like shrapnel shells and sinkholes over trench dugouts in the Palo Alto hills are vivid reminders of Camp Fremont's legacy. But the larger legacy is all around us, an inheritance of America's brief Great War.

Like a mushroom that dies but sends mycelia subtly outward, the former Camp Fremont initially remained open ground. Some units, including the remount station on Willow Road and some central warehouses, functioned until April 1920 as depots for the army's Western Department quartermaster corps at Fort Mason in San Francisco. Except for the hospital, the rest of the camp acreage reverted to its owners, including Stanford University. Camp buildings and other physical effects were sold at auction. Wooden structures went for $150. Frugal locals carried them off like packrats. A physician who bought her Menlo Park cottage in the early 1980s was tickled to learn that it consisted of two Camp Fremont structures spliced together east of Alameda de las Pulgas, on the former grounds of the Eighth Division's Sanitary Train. Santa Clara University bought the camp's sports field bleachers. The City of Palo Alto snapped up the Hostess House designed by noted architect Julia

The 319th Engineers practice their skills by building a pontoon bridge across Stanford's Felt Lake. *Menlo Park Historical Association.*

Morgan and moved it to University Avenue for use as a community center and, today, the MacArthur Park restaurant.

The brief federal subsidy that was Camp Fremont served as bridge funding for Hoag & Lansdale's Menlo Park subdivisions, as well as for other entities that had struggled before the war. Camp Fremont not only sewerized Hoag's land but also gave time for the crucial ingredient in growth to reach the area, namely, automobile ownership. In 1910, there were 36,146 passenger autos registered in California; by 1920, there were more than half a million. Menlo Park's small Presbyterian church, for example, though supported in the nineteenth century by Jane Stanford, had closed in 1916 due to poor attendance. The community was almost entirely Catholic, and the Presbytery of San Francisco proposed to sell the building and concentrate its efforts in other towns. When Camp Fremont arrived, the denomination changed its mind and used the church building for ministries to the soldiers. By 1920, Menlo Park Presbyterian Church was able to scrape together enough Protestants to open a Sunday school. By April 1920, when Camp Fremont was abandoned, Hoag's lots had begun to sell. In the census of that year, Los Angeles passed San Francisco in population, where it would remain. The "Greater San Francisco" of which Camp Fremont was a manifestation had fallen short of Mayor James Rolph's vision. Yet the seeds of the greater Bay Area's development had been planted, and they grew.

MAPPING THE FUTURE

In Camp Fremont, we can discern the beginning of the end of imperial San Francisco. We can see it in the nascent political independence of Camp Fremont's suburban neighbors, whose growing resistance to city plans such as amalgamation helped shape the maneuvering required to site the camp on the Peninsula. We can see it in the skills many Camp Fremont soldiers acquired there to help develop a suburbanizing state. We can see it in Stanford's postwar financial and administrative modernization as the university, perhaps sobered by its Camp Fremont episode, took steps that would enable it to become an intellectual engine for Silicon Valley and the world. Rolph and his peers continued to promote regional projects beyond their city's limits, including the trans-bay automobile bridges and airports such as the Moffett Naval Air Station. Yet this development was a double-edged sword for San Francisco. Though Rolph undoubtedly thought of these transportation links as conduits to stream assets into San Francisco, they of course ran both ways, and they eventually provided the means for much of the city's *contado* to become autonomous. Three generations later, San Francisco was passed in size not only by Los Angeles but also by San Jose, an agricultural town of thirty thousand during the war.

Camp Fremont's trench-field galleries became an attractive nuisance to canoodling couples and curious small boys. In 1920, some Palo Alto residents were accused by the Justice Department of stealing canned goods and other surplus from the camp and hiding them in the abandoned trenches. The ringleader was a former jitney driver who had learned about the trenches from the officers he ferried from their quarters in town to the camp. Magnetometric sensing appears to corroborate vestiges of the periphery of the trench system, including dugouts and a tunnel that connects to the Boyau of Florida just off Sand Hill Road. Today, after heavy rains, these dugouts reappear as sinkholes, and bullets wash down the creeks.

Many of the former munitions grounds remain restricted or undeveloped for various reasons: SLAC's site because it is managed under license from the federal Department of Energy; Dish Hill because it is a conservation area and because of the Cold War–era radiotelescope near its summit that gives the hill its current name; the Jasper Ridge Biological Preserve because of its ecological significance; and the City of Palo Alto's Foothills Park and Pearson-Arastradero Preserve because of the potential of human overuse. Still, the former use of these lands must be included in conversations about their development, especially because, in some cases, hazards have remained.

Despite assurances that the War Department would restore leased properties to their prewar state, the government did not comprehensively

This page: Boys prepare in 1940 to enter one of the trench ground's subterranean passages. The system was sealed soon after. *Jim Rutherford, SLAC National Accelerator Laboratory, Archives and History Office.*

clear and demine all the maneuver grounds. That task would have been huge: 400,000 pounds of lead was reportedly extracted from former Camp Fremont maneuver grounds during World War II–era scrap-metal drives. On the former artillery range, efforts are ongoing. The seventy-five-millimeter shell detonated in November 2010 near the Palo Alto Hills Golf and Country Club was found amid fragments of some sixty shells unearthed in a one- to two-acre area. Another unexploded seventy-five-millimeter shell was detonated in February 2008 off nearby Alexis Drive.

Major Dorst and Colonel Otwell were among at least 150 veterans of the 319th who relocated to the Bay Area after the war, having moved with their Defenders Club brides to Berkeley and the Barron Park neighborhood of Palo Alto, respectively. The 319th held annual reunions throughout the state until 1971. When the reunions met in Menlo Park, the engineers, fewer each time, cruised the streets with leaflets reminding them where the Camp Fremont units had been. They passed the 12th Infantry's quarters, between Oak Grove and Valparaiso Avenues, where the troops watched Sacred Heart Academy's girls' athletic games until the nuns put a stop to it. They reviewed their own unit area just to the east, where Lieutenant James Francis Quisenberry had laid out tennis courts for the officers and a circular bed in red and white foliage with a castle, symbol of the U.S. Army Corps of Engineers. Unlike the returnees, Quisenberry never made it home. He died of influenza en route to France, leaving behind an infant son he had seen only once, for a few minutes in 1918.

Attending these reunions obliged Dorst to pass Treasure Island, which he had dredged from San Francisco Bay during a later, larger war. They prompted him to reminisce:

> *The project was to build an island in the Bay by depositing dredged sand on about a square mile of submerged flat. Memories of the 319th were helpful here. The hoped-for contractors refused to bid, so* [Army] *Engineer Dept. dredges had to be mobilized and started working. Many held the job impossible due to the waves and currents. Then the cry became that the money would not be enough. The likeness to the 319th's situation years before was striking. So all that had to be done was to determine what the 319th would do in such circumstances—and then do it.*[110]

Camp Fremont existed in a unique moment in American history. The nation stood poised between rurality and urbanism, horsepower and auto power, chivalric notions of battle and industrialized war. It's tempting to see

The 319th Engineers' headquarters at Camp Fremont, with the corps' emblematic castle laid out in foliage and stone. *Menlo Park Historical Association.*

camps like Fremont as helping to tip the scales. Camp Fremont came to the San Francisco Peninsula because the people who brought it there wanted to be modern. Foremost, of course, they wanted to win what H.G. Wells called "the war to end war." They also wanted to fight disease, ignorance, disunity and the spotty infrastructure that kept many Americans, even an hour's train ride from San Francisco, living essentially nineteenth-century lives.

Intellectuals of the 1910s looked to the immediate past for inspiration, to a vanishing agrarian ideal. Yet many of the most interesting people in Camp Fremont's story believed that by embracing modernity they could change the world. Whether they drove tanks, made maps or strove to save patients in the face of an epidemic, they chose change, movement, opportunity. They were wrong about World War I being "the war to end war." We still fight wars. Yet the way the landscape has changed between our time and theirs is evidence that in many other ways they were right.

NOTES

Introduction

1. Hiram Johnson, letter to Harris Weinstock, April 16, 1917, Hiram W. Johnson Papers, BANC MSS C-B 581, Bancroft Library, University of California–Berkeley.
2. Ray Lyman Wilbur, notes dictated November 2, 1946, Ray Lyman Wilbur Personal Papers, SC 0064B, Stanford University Archives (hereafter SUA).
3. Aloe, *Twelfth U.S. Infantry*, 48.

Chapter 1

4. *Redwood City Democrat*, April 19, 1917, 3.
5. Rosen, *Lost Sisterhood*, 16–17, 28.
6. Kazin, *Barons of Labor*, 200.
7. *San Francisco Chronicle*, November 24, 1917, 1; October 2, 1917, 1.
8. Letter from J.S. Dunnigan to adjutant, Western Department, RG 165, NARA.
9. *Redwood City Democrat*, March 1, 1917, 2.
10. Letter from William Bowers Bourn to Edward J. McCutcheon, August 5, 1918, Spring Valley Water Co. Papers, BANC MSS C-G 189, Bancroft Library.
11. Edward F. O'Day, *Wartime Activities of William Bowers Bourn* [1923?], SC 793, SUA.

12. Wilbur, notes dictated November 2, 1946. Wilbur Papers, SUA.
13. *Daily Palo Alto* (later *Stanford Daily*), April 18, 1917, 1+; "Memoranda Theodore Roosevelt," undated [1919], Wilbur Papers, SUA.
14. *New York Times*, January 31, 1915, 6; *Stanford Illustrated Review*, March 1917, 5; *Daily Palo Alto*, April 18, 1917, 1+; Mirrielees, *Stanford*, 183–84.
15. *Camp Fremont* (Menlo Park, CA: Harry C. Freeman, 1918).
16. "Beautiful Menlo Park," brochure published by Hoag & Lansdale, 1908.
17. Letter from Dunnigan.
18. Timothy Hopkins, telegram to James D. Phelan, July 19, 1917, Charles D. Marx Papers, SC 0161, SUA.
19. Letter from Walter Hoag to Major William Bramstedt, Camp Fremont, April 10, 1919, RG 393, NARA.
20. *Stanford Illustrated Review*, October 1917, 11+.
21. *San Francisco Chronicle*, December 1, 1917, 4; December 5, 1917, 4; *San Francisco Chamber of Commerce Activities* 4, no. 48 (November 29, 1917): 305; *San Francisco Chronicle*, November 23, 1917, 9.
22. *San Francisco Chronicle*, November 23, 1917, 9.
23. Ibid., October 2, 1917, 9; Rolph 1917 daybook 235, San Francisco History Center, San Francisco Public Library.
24. *San Francisco Chronicle*, October 2, 1917, 9.
25. Ibid., December 7, 1917, 7.

Chapter 2

26. Hunter Liggett, letter to Stanford Board of Trustees, July 27, 1917, Meeting Records of the Board of Trustees, SC 1010, SUA.
27. *Argonaut* 81, no. 2110 (September 1, 1917): 130.
28. Letter from J.M. Stillman to Ray Lyman Wilbur, July 25, 1917; letter, Wilbur to Stillman, August 2, 1917; telegram, Wilbur to Marx, August 9, 1918, all Wilbur Papers, SUA.
29. *Argonaut* 95, no. 2430 (June 27, 1931): 18.
30. Creel, *How We Advertised America*, 16–17; Eustace Cullinan, "War Savings and Thrift," *San Francisco Chamber of Commerce Activities* 5, no. 15 (April 11, 1918): 9.
31. *Sunset Magazine*'s "New San Francisco Emergency Edition," www.sfmuseum.org/sunset/magazine.html.
32. Letter from R.M. Hotaling to commanding officer, Camp Fremont, February 19, 1918, RG 393 Part V Entry 1, NARA.

33. Letter from Hiram Johnson to C.K. McClatchy, May 15, 1918, Johnson Papers.
34. *Collier's* 59, no. 6 (April 21, 1917): 12–13; *San Francisco Chamber of Commerce Activities* 4, no. 37 (September 13, 1917): 201.
35. *Collier's* 59, no. 10 (May 19, 1917): 48; 61, no. 24 (August 24, 1918): 13.
36. *Trench and Camp*, April 27, 1918, 8; *Redwood City Tribune*, April 29, 1918, 1.
37. *Congressional Record*, April 24, 1918, Senate 5546; May 4, 1918, Senate 6037.
38. Grotelueschen, *AEF Way of War*, 350; Faulkner, *School of Hard Knocks*, 316.
39. Elliott, *It Happened This Way*, 323.
40. Ibid., 310–11, 313–14; *San Francisco Chronicle*, May 24, 1918, 1; June 2, 1918, 1.
41. Elliott, *It Happened This Way*, 315–21.
42. Ibid., 322.
43. *Annual Report 1917–18*, 17; *Daily Palo Alto*, May 21, 1917, 2; November 5, 1917, 1+; Minutes of the Academic Council, January 4, 1918, 185; *Annual Report*, 1917–18, 42; *Daily Palo Alto*, November 6, 1918, 1; Wilbur and Edwards, *Memoirs of Wilbur*, 245, 247; *Congressional Record*, April 24, 1918, Senate 5546.
44. Mirrielees, *Stanford*, 188; *Stanford Illustrated Review*, May 1918, 287.
45. Hotaling and Sterling, *Twilight of the Kings*, 53.

Chapter 3

46. Letters from Muriel Hamilton to unknown recipient(s), June 17, June 22, June 25, June 30, 1918; August 8, 1918; September 12, September 29, 1918; October 20, 1918; November 4, 1918; all Helen Athey Collection 306-87, MPHA.
47. *Stanford Daily*, March 14, 1918.
48. Bristow, *Making Men Moral*, 16, 246.
49. Letters from Harriet Bradford to R.L. Wilbur, August 30, 1917, November 16, 1917, both in Ray Lyman Wilbur Presidential Papers, SC 0064A, SUA.
50. Mann, *Mishpucah*, 108–9; *Redwood City Democrat*, July 19, 1917, 1.
51. Kennedy, *Progressivism*, 138.
52. Case 8000-328367, Case 320588, Investigative Case Files of the Bureau of Investigation 1908–22, M1085, NARA.
53. Case 172947, M1085, NARA.

54. Memo from D.O. Lively to Eastern Division Personnel, dated "New Year 1920," American National Red Cross Records, Hoover Institution Archives, Stanford; Neiberg, *World War I Reader*, 291.
55. *New York Times*, December 2, 1933.
56. Letter from D.O. Lively to Major H.L. Bridges, April 2, 1920, American National Red Cross Records.
57. Letter from D.O. Lively to acting commissioner, Siberian Commission, May 25, 1920, American National Red Cross Records.
58. Reginald T. Townsend, "Tanks and the Hose of Death," in *The World's Work*, ed. Arthur W. Page, 33, no. 2 (December 1916): 204–5.
59. McMaster, *Ultimate Sacrifice*, 35–36.
60. Ibid., 38.
61. *Collier's* 61, no. 1 (March 16, 1918): 12.

Chapter 4

62. Letter from Charles J. Sullivan to Rowena Gray, October 15, 1918, SSC 962, SUA.
63. *Collier's* 61, no. 13 (June 1, 1918): 11+; 62, no. 12 (November 30, 1918): 22.
64. Letter from Captain William Potter to Colonel E.B. Frick, commander, Medical Corps, May 1, 1918, RG 112, NARA.
65. Bristow, *Making Men Moral*, xvii; *Keeping Fit to Fight*, Commission on Training Camp Activities 5.
66. *Carry On*, Commission on Training Camp Activities 5.
67. Aloe, *Twelfth U.S. Infantry*, 183; letter from Major Charles H. Stearns, Medical Corps, to Major William Brandstedt, QM Corps, October 26, 1918, RG 112, NARA.
68. Aloe, *Twelfth U.S. Infantry*, 62, 75, 278–79.
69. Memo from Private Harry Gottesfeld, HQ, Camp Fremont to Captain Little, December 1, 1918, RG 393, NARA; Weed, *Military Hospitals*, 109, 664–66.
70. *New York Times*, April 4, 1919; letter from Orval Rasor to Hazel Rasor, September 29, 1918, Hazel Rasor Collection, SC 306-87a, Menlo Park Historical Association (hereafter MPHA).
71. Weed, *Military Hospitals*, 109.
72. Aloe, *Twelfth U.S. Infantry*, 287.
73. *Collier's* 61, no. 10 (May 18, 1918): 16+; 59, no. 21 (August 4, 1917): 11; 61, no. 19 (July 20, 1918): 9+.

74. Letter from Colonel S.E. Smiley to commanding general, Western Department, November 6, 1917, RG 395, NARA; memorandum from Colonel E.B. Frick, Medical Corps, May 13, 1918, RG 112, NARA.
75. Proceedings of a Board of Officers convened at Camp Fremont, pursuant to Special Orders No. 126, September 13, 1918, RG 112, NARA; letter from Camp Fremont fire marshal to commanding general, February 5, 1918, RG 395, NARA; Aloe, *Twelfth U.S. Infantry*, 135.
76. Letter from Captain William D. Potter, QM, to Fremont base commander, September 13, 1918, RG 112, NARA.
77. Opdycke, *Flu Epidemic*, 2; Crosby, *America's Forgotten Pandemic*, 25; Byerly, "U.S. Military and the Influenza Pandemic," 90.
78. Letter from Colonel F.F. Russell to Camp Fremont base hospital commander, September 26, 1918, RG 112, NARA.
79. General Order 18, October 8, 1918; General Order 19, October 9, 1918, both RG 393, NARA; Aloe, *Twelfth U.S. Infantry*, 138–40; report of Major Walter V. Brem, MD, *Pandemic Influenza and Secondary Pneumonia at Camp Fremont*, RG 112, NARA.
80. Aloe, *Twelfth U.S. Infantry*, 143, 223, 274.
81. Ibid., 55, 138–40, 227.
82. Brem, *Pandemic Influenza*; letter from Charles J. Sullivan to Rowena Gray, October 8, 1918, Sullivan Papers, SUA.
83. Brem, *Pandemic Influenza.*
84. Letter from L.L. Smith to surgeon general HQ, October 16, 1918, RG 112, NARA.
85. Letters from Charles J. Sullivan to Rowena Gray, October 10, 12, 14, 1918, Sullivan Papers, SUA.
86. Aloe, *Twelfth U.S. Infantry*, 55, 62, 129.
87. Ibid., 126.
88. Bristow, *American Pandemic*, 9–10, 119–21; Aloe, *Twelfth U.S. Infantry*, vi–vii, 216, 226, 230, 328, 424.
89. Aloe, *Twelfth U.S. Infantry*, 58–59, 287; Crowell and Wilson, *How America Went to War*, 99–100.
90. Brem, *Pandemic Influenza.*
91. Letter from Lieutenant Herbert L. Williams to chief of engineers, AEF, December 1, 1918, RG 120, NARA.
92. Crosby, *America's Forgotten Pandemic*, 130; Spears, "On the Roll of Honor," 7, 9–14.
93. Letter from Lieutenant August L. Barreau to chief of engineers, AEF, December 10, 1918, RG 120, NARA; letter from Lieutenant Charles

L. Burton to chief of engineers, AEF, December 13, 1918; letter from Captain David S. Ferguson to chief of engineers, AEF, December 10, 1918, RG 120, NARA; *New York Times*, April 4, 1919.
94. Letter from Ferguson to chief of engineers; Crosby, *America's Forgotten Pandemic*, 123–25, 140; March, *Nation at War*, 93.
95. Crosby, *America's Forgotten Pandemic*, 136.
96. Letter from Barreau to chief of engineers.
97. Letter from Lieutenant Charles L. Burton to chief of engineers, AEF, December 13, 1918, RG 120, NARA.
98. Letter from Major L.D. Worsham to chief of engineers, AEF, December 9, 1918, RG 120, NARA.
99. Letter from Captain W.L. Harwell to chief of engineers, AEF, December 1, 1918; letter from Lieutenant Edward S. Rothchild to chief of engineers, AEF, both RG 120, NARA.
100. Letter from Lieutenant D.E.A. Cameron to chief of engineers, AEF, November 30, 1918, RG 120, NARA; letter from Rothchild to chief of engineers.
101. Letter from Barreau to chief of engineers; letter from Lieutenant Watson B. Joyes to chief of engineers, AEF, December 13, 1918, RG 120, NARA.

Chapter 5

102. Letter from Barreau to chief of engineers.
103. Captain H.F. Taylor, "History of the 319th Engineer Regiment," RG 120, NARA.
104. Aloe, *Twelfth U.S. Infantry*, 243–44.
105. Keegan, *First World War*, 313–16.
106. Faulkner, *School of Hard Knocks*, 84, 277, 320.
107. Chasseaud, *Rats Alley*, 29.
108. Taylor, "History of the 319th Engineer Regiment"; "Personal History, James Archer Dorst, August 4, 1971," Johnston Family Collection, SC 130, MPHA.
109. Anthony, "Memorial of Maxwell Naylor Short," 309–12.
110. "Personal History, James Archer Dorst."

BIBLIOGRAPHY

Archival Sources

Bancroft Library, University of California–Berkeley. Hiram Johnson Papers, MSS C-B 581.
———. Spring Valley Water Co. Papers, MSS C-G 189.
California Historical Society, San Francisco. James Rolph Jr. Papers.
Department of Special Collections and University Archives, Stanford University Libraries. Berton W. Crandall Proof Album, PC003.
———. Charles D. Marx Papers, SC0161.
———. Charles J. Sullivan Letters, SC0962.
———. Francis William Bergstrom Scrapbook, SC866.
———. Meeting Records of the Board of Trustees, 1908, 1916–17, 1917–18, SC1010.
———. President Ray Lyman Wilbur Papers, SC0064A.
———. Ray Lyman Wilbur Personal Papers, SC0064B.
———. R.E. Swain Papers, SC0039.
———. Stanford War Records, SC0019.
Menlo Park Historical Association, Menlo Park, California.
National Archives, Washington, D.C.
San Francisco History Center, San Francisco Public Library. James Rolph Papers.

BIBLIOGRAPHY

Published and Manuscript Sources

Aloe, Alfred. *Twelfth U.S. Infantry 1798–1919: Its Story—By Its Men*. New York: Knickerbocker Press, 1919.

Ames, Katherine. "Tete-a-Tete." *The Trident of Delta Delta Delta*, November 1917.

Annual Report of the President, 1917–18. Stanford, CA: Stanford University, 1918.

Annual Report of the President, 1918–19. Stanford, CA: Stanford University, 1919.

Anthony, John W. "Memorial of Maxwell Naylor Short." *Amer Mineralogist* 38, no. 4 (March–April 1953): 309–12.

Barbeau, Arthur A., and Florette Henri. *The Unknown Soldiers: Black American Troops in World War I*. Philadelphia: Temple University Press, 1974.

Bocek, Barbara, and Elena Reese. *Land Use History of Jasper Ridge Biological Preserve*. Stanford, CA: Jasper Ridge Biological Preserve Research Report 8, August 15, 1992.

Brechin, Gray. *Imperial San Francisco: Urban Power, Earthly Ruin*. Berkeley: University of California Press, 1999.

Bristow, Nancy K. *American Pandemic: The Lost Worlds of the 1918 Influenza Epidemic*. New York: Oxford University Press, 2012.

———. *Making Men Moral: Social Engineering During the Great War*. New York: New York University Press, 1996.

Byerly, Carol R. "The U.S. Military and the Influenza Pandemic of 1918–1919." *Public Health Rep. 2010* (Suppl 3).

Camp Fremont Artillery Target Range. From Instrumental Survey by 319th Engineers 8th Division (Regular). N.d. [1918]. Map. Records of the Historical Section, RG 165 NM-84 Entry 310, NARA.

Camp Fremont Trench Maneuver Ground. From Instrumental Survey by 319th Engineers 8th Division (Regular). May 1918. Map. Records of the Historical Section, RG 165 NM-84 Entry 310, NARA.

Chaffey, J.B. "Completion Report of Construction Operations at Camp Fremont." Typescript in collection of the U.S. Army Military History Institute, Carlisle, PA, n.d. [1918].

Chasseaud, Peter. *Artillery's Astrologers: A History of British Survey and Mapping on the Western Front 1914–1918*. London: Clearaway Logistics Operations, 1999.

———. *Rats Alley: Trench Names of the Western Front, 1914–1918*. London: Spellmount, 2006.

Clemmer, Heather A. "The City That Knows How: San Francisco, The Great War, and Urban Identity." Diss., University of Oklahoma, 2008.

Coffman, Edward M. *The War to End All Wars: The American Military Experience in World War I*. New York: Oxford University Press, 1968.

BIBLIOGRAPHY

Creel, George. *How We Advertised America*. New York: Harper and Bros., 1920.

Crook, Nigel. "Camp Fremont Trench Maneuver Ground: 1918 Map with Contemporary Google Earth Overlay." 2010. PDF file.

———. "SLAC—Geophysical Survey Summary: Arch115/315 Class Exercise." November 18, 2010. PowerPoint presentation.

Crosby, Alfred W. *America's Forgotten Pandemic: The Influenza of 1918*. 2nd ed. Cambridge, UK: Cambridge University Press, 2003.

Crowell, Benedict, and Robert Forrest Wilson. *How America Went to War: An Account from Official Sources of the Nation's War Activities, 1917–20*. Vol. 2, *The Road to France*. New Haven, CT: Yale University Press, 1921.

Duniway, C.A. "War History of Stanford." Stanford War Records, Stanford University Archives. December 1938.

Elliott, Ellen Coit. *It Happened This Way*. Stanford, CA: Stanford University Press, 1940.

Farwell, Byron. *Over There: The United States in the Great War, 1917–18*. New York: Norton, 1999.

Faulkner, Richard S. *The School of Hard Knocks*. College Station: Texas A&M University Press, 2012.

Flanagan, Maureen. *America Reformed: Progressives and Progressivisms, 1890s–1920s*. Oxford University Press, 2007.

Grotelueschen, Mark Ethan. *The AEF Way of War: The American Army and Combat in World War I*. New York: Cambridge University Press, 2007.

Gruber, Carol S. *Mars and Minerva: World War I and the Uses of the Higher Learning in America*. Baton Rouge: University of Louisiana Press, 1975.

Harbaugh, Dwight W. Interview with the author, November 4, 2011.

———. "1948 Aerial Photograph of Area West of Main Gate (with 2010 USGS Overlay Pointing to 1948 Topographic Anomalies and 1990 Sinkhole)." National Accelerator Laboratory Environmental Protection Department, November 2011. PDF file.

Hart, Alfred Bushnell, ed. *Harper's Pictorial History of the World War*. Vol. 5, *The United States in the War*. New York: Harper and Brothers, 1920.

Hauser, Caleb. Interview with the author, December 15, 2011.

Helfrich, Frank. Interview with the author, September 20, 2011.

Hotaling, Richard M., and George Sterling. *Twilight of the Kings: A Masque of Democracy*. San Francisco: Bohemian Grove Publishing, 1918.

Infantry Training. Washington, D.C.: Army War College, 1918.

Instructions for the Defensive Combat of Small Units. Washington, D.C.: U.S. Department of War, 1918.

BIBLIOGRAPHY

Jacks, Noel H. "The Story of Camp Fremont." Memorial Number, *Daily Palo Alto Times*, n.d. [1919?], 5–8.

Jones, Linda. Interview with the author, September 23, 2011.

Jordan, David Starr. *The Days of a Man*. Vol. 2, *1900–1921*. Yonkers-on-Hudson, NY: World Book Co., 1922.

Kazin, Michael. *Barons of Labor: The S.F. Building Trades and Union Power in the Progressive Era*. Urbana: University of Illinois Press, 1987.

Keegan, John. *The First World War*. New York: Knopf, 1999.

Kennedy, David. *Over Here: The First World War and American Society*. New York: Oxford University Press, 1980.

———. *Progressivism: The Critical Issues*. Boston: Little, Brown, 1971.

Kimber, Arthur Clifford. *The Story of the First Flag*. San Francisco: Friends of France, 1920.

Lands of Leland Stanford Junior University in the Counties of Santa Clara and San Mateo. Map. Stanford, CA: Stanford University, 1940.

Lawrence, Jerry, and Brian Bondurant. "War Relics in the Valley of Heart's Delight." *Foothills Nature Notes*. City of Palo Alto Community Services Department, Open Space, Parks and Golf Division, n.d. [1995?].

Mann, Louise Henriques. *The Mishpucah: Growing Up Jewish in Early Palo Alto*. Victoria, BC: Saturna Publishing, 2003.

March, Peyton. *The Nation at War*. Garden City, NY: Doubleday, 1932.

McMaster, Gary. *The Ultimate Sacrifice*. Camp Roberts, CA: Camp Roberts Historical Association, 2008.

Miele, Martin J., Norcal Geophysical Consultants, Inc. Letter to Gordon I. Ratcliff, SLAC, April 30, 1990.

Mirrielees, Edith R. *Stanford: The Story of a University*. New York: Putnam, 1959.

Nash, George H. *Herbert Hoover and Stanford University*. Stanford, CA: Hoover Institution Press, 1988.

Neiberg, Michael S., ed. *The World War I Reader*. New York: New York University Press, 2007.

Nye, Wilbur Sturtevant. *Carbine and Lance: The Story of Old Fort Sill*. Norman: University of Oklahoma Press, 1969.

Opdycke, Sandra. *The Flu Epidemic of 1918: America's Experience in the Global Health Crisis*. New York: Routledge, 2014.

Page, Arthur W. *Our 110 Days' Fighting*. New York: Doubleday, 1920.

Palo Alto Online News. "Big Midnight Bang in Foothills Was WWI Shell." February 7, 2008.

Pelling, Dick, USA Environmental, Inc., Oldsmar, FL. E-mail to Caleb Hauser of Tincher Construction Co., Redwood City, CA, December 9, 2011.

BIBLIOGRAPHY

Peterson, Christina. "Rangers Find World War I Shell in Park." *San Jose Mercury News*, February 8, 2008, B1.

Rosen, Ruth. *The Lost Sisterhood: Prostitution in America 1900–1918*. Baltimore, MD: Johns Hopkins University Press, 1983.

Showalter, William Joseph. "America's New Soldier Cities." *National Geographic*, November 1917, 439–76.

Smith, R.L., and G.A. Elliott. "Map of Menlo Park and Vicinity Showing Areas, Boundary Lines and Ownerships of the Several Tracts of Land Constituting the Government Reservation for Camp Fremont Base Hospital and Remount Depot." February 1918.

Snyder, John P. "Map Projections: A Working Manual." U.S. Geological Survey Professional Paper 1395. Washington, D.C.: Government Printing Office, 1987.

Spears, George M. "On the Roll of Honor: First Lieutenant James Francis Quisenberry, Company E, 319th Engineers, United States Army." *Register of Kentucky State Historical Society* 17, no. 50 (May 1919): 7, 9–14.

Stanford Illustrated Review. "At Our Gates." May 1918, 287.

———. "Fremont, The Flirt." October 1917, 11+.

Strobridge, William S. *Golden Gate to Golden Horn: Camp Fremont, Calif., and the American Experience in Siberia of 1918*. San Mateo, CA: San Mateo County Historical Association, n.d. [1973?].

Svanevik, Michael. *Menlo Park: Beyond the Gate*. N.p.: Menlo Park Historical Association, 2000.

Swanson, Robert. *Domestic United States Military Facilities of the First World War 1917–1919: A Postal History*. Rapid City, SD, 2010.

Thwing, Charles Franklin. *The American Colleges and Universities in the Great War: A History*. New York: Macmillan, 1920.

Weed, Frank W. *Military Hospitals in the United States*. Vol. 5 (1923), *The Medical Department of the United States Army in the World War*. Edited by Charles Lynch, Frank W. Weed and Loy McAfee. Washington, D.C.: U.S. Army Surgeon General's Office, 1923–29.

Wheeler, Benjamin Ide. *War Service Record for the Academic Year 1917–1918*. Berkeley: University of California Press, 1918.

Wilbur, Ray Lyman, and Paul Carroll Edwards. *The Memoirs of Ray Lyman Wilbur, 1875–1949*. Stanford, CA: Stanford University Press, 1960.

Worthen, James. *Governor James Rolph and the Great Depression in California*. Jefferson, NC: McFarland and Co., 2006.

INDEX

A

alcohol 75
  Prohibition 25
American Protective League 75
artillery range at Camp Fremont 8, 14, 45, 46, 50, 54, 55, 56, 57, 59, 114, 121, 127
Atherton 35

B

Baker, Newton D. 13, 29, 35, 65, 66, 92
Bohemian Club 51, 68
Bourn, William Bowers, II 17, 20, 24, 27, 28, 29
Brechin, Gray 12, 24
Bristow, Nancy 87, 102
Britton, John A. 24, 34, 38, 40, 43

C

Commission on Training Camp Activities 31, 65, 74, 87, 89, 97, 101
Committee on Public Information (CPI) 42, 43, 50, 55, 56, 84
Creel, George 42, 43, 50, 56
Croly, Herbert 27

D

de Young, M.H. 20, 24, 34, 41
Dorst, James A. 74, 122, 127
Dumbarton Bridge 19, 26, 36

E

Eastman, Sam 24, 28, 38
Elliott, Ellen 62, 63, 64

F

Faulkner, Richard 54, 61, 115
Fitzpatrick, E.F. 26, 27, 33
Frémont, John C. 34, 38

G

Germany 8, 18, 21, 27, 29, 52, 63, 99, 115, 118, 120

H

Hoag, Walter 24, 32, 33, 34, 35, 36, 40, 61, 124
  Hoag & Lansdale 32, 34, 124

INDEX

Hoover, Herbert 13, 29, 31, 55, 67, 77
Hotaling, Richard M. 50, 51, 52, 53, 54, 55, 57, 59, 62, 64, 68, 114

I

influenza 16, 69, 94
  and mobilization 102, 103, 104, 105
  arrival at Camp Fremont 96
  death toll at Camp Fremont 97, 103
  quarantine 96, 97, 101, 102
  treatment 71, 99, 100

J

Johnson, Hiram 11, 53, 58, 92
Jordan, David Starr 12, 13, 31

K

Kimber, Arthur 63, 64, 67, 112

L

Liberty Loans 43
Lively, D.O. 77, 78, 82

M

maps and mapping 120, 123
Marx, Charles D. 32, 35, 47, 49, 66
Menlo Park 7, 14, 32, 33, 34, 35, 36, 47, 57, 83, 84, 89, 93, 102, 113, 123, 124, 127
metric system 54, 112, 120, 121, 123
Meuse-Argonne offensive 54, 80, 81, 82, 90, 94
Mirrielees, Edith 31, 67

N

National Guard 21, 34, 38, 40, 45, 59, 83, 90
nurses 5, 70, 71, 84, 87, 88, 89, 90, 99, 100, 105

O

Otwell, Curtis 74, 107, 122, 127

P

Palo Alto 7, 8, 29, 32, 33, 41, 47, 54, 57, 70, 71, 74, 75, 76, 93, 96, 97, 98, 113, 115, 123, 125, 127
Panama-Pacific International Exposition 12, 19, 21, 28, 29, 77
Phelan, James D. 33, 35

R

Red Cross 39
  overseas service 77, 78
Redwood City 26, 34, 53, 57
Roberts, Harold W. 79, 80, 82, 94, 112
Rolph, James, Jr. 17, 18, 19, 21, 24, 25, 26, 27, 33, 34, 36, 37, 38, 40, 41, 43, 45, 124, 125

S

sex 64, 69, 74
  and venereal disease 11, 73, 87
Siberia 8, 68, 71, 78, 101
Spring Valley Water Co. 24, 27, 28, 29, 30, 33, 38, 41, 92
Stanford Linear Accelerator Center (SLAC) 8, 112, 125
Stanford University
  Dish Hill 8, 50
Stern, Rosalie 84, 100

T

319th Engineers 14, 45, 55, 74, 93, 103, 105, 110, 111, 112, 117, 118, 120
training camps
  Bowie 83
  Fort Sill (Doniphan) 10, 58, 59, 62
  Funston (Fort Riley) 94
  Kearny 24, 38, 57, 92
  Lewis 24, 38, 71, 121
  Mills 91, 103
  Upton 96, 103
Twelfth Infantry Regiment 14, 93, 97, 101, 102, 103, 114, 117, 127

INDEX

U

University of California–Berkeley 17, 57, 63, 66

W

Wilbur, Ray Lyman 12, 17, 20, 24, 26, 29, 30, 31, 47, 49, 66, 92, 111
Wilson, Woodrow 8, 11, 13, 21, 33, 40, 53, 58, 63, 66, 67, 92, 99, 105

ABOUT THE AUTHOR

Barbara Wilcox is a longtime journalist and writer in news, public affairs and American culture. Her interest in World War I dates to tales told by her grandfather, who served with the American Expeditionary Force's 319th Services of Supply in Gironde, France. This book was inspired during her term as a writer for the U.S. Geological Survey in Menlo Park, California, when USGS geophysicists proposed testing magnetometers over "Stanford's hidden World War I tunnels." It originated in a question no one seemed able to answer: why were the tunnels there? The Stanford Historical Society awarded Wilcox its Prize for Excellence in Historical Writing for research that led to this book. Barbara Wilcox is a graduate of the University of California–Berkeley and Stanford University. She lives in Menlo Park, on the site of Camp Fremont's school for bakers and cooks.